THE Delaware ADVENTURE

Dr. Barbara E. Benson
Dr. Carol E. Hoffecker

Gibbs Smith, Publisher
Salt Lake City

ABOUT THE AUTHORS

Dr. Barbara E. Benson received her B.A. in history from Beloit College and her Ph.D. from Indiana University. She came to Delaware on what was supposed to be a short-term position at the Hagley Museum and Library and immediately came to love the history and culture of the First State. Now, more than 30 years later, she continues to study, write, and teach about her adopted state.

Dr. Benson recently retired as director of the Historical Society of Delaware. While at the Society, she served as managing editor of *Delaware History* magazine and helped create its "hands-on history" programs for schools and the exhibition "Distinctively Delaware." She has also been an adjunct professor of history at the University of Delaware for many years, teaching courses in American and Delaware history.

A publisher of books and articles on state and local history, Dr. Benson has also served on boards of preservation, archival, museum, and civic organizations. She has been a frequent lecturer at teacher's workshops, civic organizations, and historical societies throughout the state. She currently serves as chair of the New Castle County Historic Review Board.

Dr. Carol E. Hoffecker is a native Delawarean. After graduating from the University of Delaware with a major in history, she earned a Ph.D. from Harvard University. She then returned to Delaware, where she worked for several years on the staff of the Hagley Museum and Library before joining the faculty of the University of Delaware. She recently retired as the Richards Professor of History.

Dr. Hoffecker is the author of *Wilmington, Delaware: Portrait of an Industrial City, Corporate Capital: Wilmington in the Twentieth Century, Honest John Williams, U.S. Senator from Delaware,* and *Democracy in Delaware: the Story of the First State's General Assembly.* Her book, *Delaware, the First State,* has been used as a reader in many of the state's schools.

Dr. Hoffecker has also served as an exhibit curator or consultant to historical institutions, including the Historical Society of Delaware, the Delaware Public Archives, and the Rockwood Museum. She is editor of the magazine, *Delaware History.*

Copyright © 2007 by Gibbs Smith, Publisher
All rights reserved. No part of this book may be reproduced by any means whatsoever, either mechanical or electronic, without permission from the publisher.

Published by
Gibbs Smith, Publisher
P.O. Box 667
Layton, UT 84041
800-748-5439
www.gibbs-smith.com/textbooks

Managing Editor: Susan A. Myers
Associate Editors: Carrie Gibson, Valerie Hatch, Jennifer Petersen, Courtney Thomas
Photo Editor: Janis J. Hansen
Book Designer: Jeremy C. Munns

Cover painting: "A Rehoboth Beach Memory,"
© Paul McGehee
A Seaside Holiday at the Delaware Shore in the Summer of 1925

Printed and bound in China
ISBN 10 : 1-58685-747-9
ISBN 13 : 978-1-58685-747-9
12 11 10   10 9 8 7 6 5 4

CONTRIBUTORS

Dr. Peter B. Mires, adjunct assistant Professor of Geography at the University of Delaware, also teaches online courses for the Virginia Community College System. Dr. Mires grew up in Dover, earned his B.A. from the University of New Hampshire, his M.A. from the University of Arkansas, and his Ph.D. from Louisiana State University.

Dr. Bonnie Meszaros, Associate Director for the Center for Economic Education and Entrepreneurship at the University of Delaware, teaches classes on economics and how to teach it. She served as project director for the *Voluntary National Content Standards* in Economics. She is a past president of the National Association of Economic Educators and holds a B.A. in History from Ohio Wesleyan University and a Ph.D. in Curriculum from the University of Delaware.

Barbara Emery, Program Coordinator for the Center for Economic Education and Entrepreneurship at the University of Delaware, taught high school economics for over 30 years before joining the Center. Ms. Emery received an undergraduate degree in history education and masters in economic education and entrepreneurship from the University of Delaware. She teaches economics classes and workshops for teachers on how to teach economics and recently designed a curriculum for a high school course on personal finance.

♪♩♪ State Song ♫♪

Our state song describes all three of our state's beautiful counties.

Our Delaware

Written by George B. Hynson; Music by Will M. S. Brown

First Verse:
Oh the hills of dear New Castle,
And the smiling vales between,
When the corn is all in tassel,
And the meadowlands are green;
Where the cattle crop the clover,
And its breath is in the air,
While the sun is shining over
Our beloved Delaware.

Chorus:
Oh our Delaware! Our beloved Delaware!
For the sun is shining over our beloved Delaware,
Oh our Delaware! Our beloved Delaware!
Here's the loyal son that pledges,
Faith to good old Delaware.

Second Verse:
Where the wheat fields break and billow,
In the peaceful land of Kent,
Where the toiler seeks his pillow,
With the blessings of content;
Where the bloom that tints the peaches,
Cheeks of merry maidens share,
And the woodland chorus preaches
A rejoicing Delaware.

Chorus

Third Verse:
Dear old Sussex visions linger,
Of the holly and the pine,
Of Henlopen's jeweled finger,
Flashing out across the brine;
Of the gardens and the hedges,
And the welcome waiting there,
For the loyal son that pledges
Faith to good old Delaware.

Chorus

Fourth Verse:
From New Castle's rolling meadows,
Through the fair rich fields of Kent,
To the Sussex shores hear echoes,
Of the pledge we now present;
Liberty and Independence,
We will guard with loyal care,
And hold fast to freedom's presence,
In our home state Delaware.

The DELAWARE Adventure

Contents

1. Delaware in the World 2
2. The First People 22
3. Explorers and Settlers from Europe 46
4. Creating a New Nation 76
5. Life and Work in the New State 102
6. Delaware in the Civil War 132
7. Into a New Century 160
8. Delaware in Modern Times 188
9. Government for the Nation and the State 214
10. Economics for Everyone 232

Maps 252
Glossary 256
Index 260
Image Credits . . . 265

Maps, Graphs, and Tables

Where in the World Are We? 6
Delaware and the Delmarva Peninsula 9
Delaware's Rivers 10
The Atlantic Flyway 13
Delaware's Largest Cities and Communities 15
Delaware's Average Temperatures and Precipitation 18
North American Indian Groups 27
Where Is Europe? 48
Searching for a Route to Asia, 1400s 50

Europeans Claim the Land 54
Bordering States 64
Triangular Trade 70
The Thirteen Colonies 78
Land Claims Before the French and Indian War 79
Where Is Philadelphia? 83
Caesar Rodney's Ride 86
Route of English Soldiers 91
Surrender at Yorktown 94
From Sea to Shining Sea 108
Delaware Railroads 123
Population, 1790–1860 131
United States, 1854 142
Delaware Population in 1860 143
United States, 1861 144
A Nation Divided—the Civil War 146
Population, 1870–1910 187
Route of DuPont Highway 194
Delaware's General Assembly 222
Counties and County Seats 225
Port of Wilmington 246

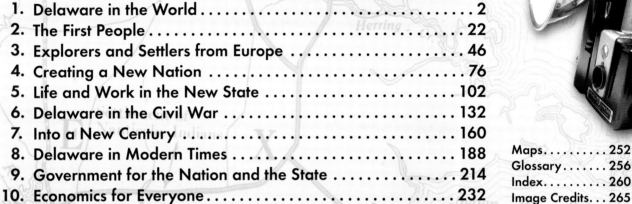

Rehoboth Beach and Boardwalk

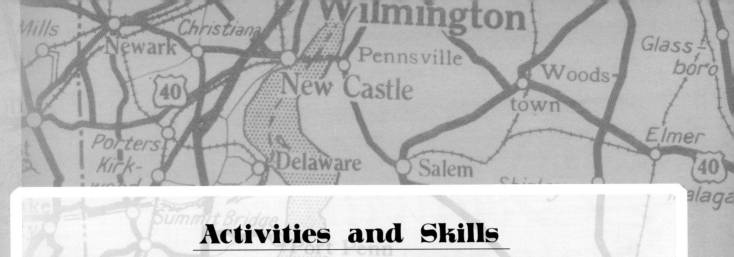

Activities and Skills

Reading a Map 8
Mental Maps 20
The Ways We Use Water 20
Compare Climates of the World 21
Where Do Delaware's People Live? 21
Indian Place Names 45
Just for Fun—Indian Games 45
Primary Source—William Penn's Letter 75
Draw a Picture of Washington's Visit 101
From Sea to Shining Sea 108
Aletta Clarke's Trip to Philadelphia, 1790 118
Inventions Make Life Easier 130
Population Graph 131
The Underground Railroad 140
Hardly Worth Eating 148

The Power of a Book 159
Write and Draw About the Civil War 159
Design a Can Label 186
Population, 1870–1910 187
The World in Your Closet 187
Connecting Cities Today 194
Role Play 212
What If? 213
Research, Write, and Draw 213
Your Local Government 225
The Preamble to the U.S. Constitution 230
Discuss Current Events 231
Visit a Government Building 231
Make a Government Bulletin Board 231
We Are All Connected 250

Lockerman Street, Dover

Rehoboth Bay

State Marine Animal:
Horseshoe Crab

Delaware Bay is home to more horseshoe crabs than any other place in the world. The small crabs are the main food for shore birds.

Delaware
State Symbols

Delaware's symbols tell us something about our state. Learn about them and tell your friends and family what they mean.

State Flower:
Peach Blossom

There were once almost one million peach trees in Delaware. Can you imagine how beautiful the trees looked when all the blossoms came out in the spring?

State Star:
Delaware Diamond

The Delaware Diamond, located in the constellation of Ursa Major (Great Bear), can be seen with binoculars or a telescope.

State Tree:
American Holly

Hollies grow well in Delaware's sandy soil. Farm families in Sussex County used to make extra money at Christmas selling holly wreaths.

State Bug:
Lady Bug

A second grade class wanted the lady bug to be our state bug. The children said the little red bugs are very helpful because they eat small insects that damage our crops.

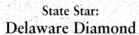

State Soil:
Greenwich Loam

The rich soil is found in all our state's counties and is important to our agriculture, wildlife habitat, and natural beauty.

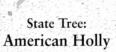

State Fish:
Weakfish

State Mineral:
Sillimanite

State Beverage:
Milk

State Bird:
Blue Hen
Delaware's soldiers carried the fighting birds with them in the Revolutionary War. They were tough birds who won most of their fights, just as Delaware's soldiers did.

Delaware's State Flag, Colors, Motto, and Nicknames

Our state seal in the center of the flag is used to mark important government papers. It shows a soldier and a farmer, a ship, a cow, corn, and wheat. Below them is the state's motto, "Liberty and Independence." You can see a close-up picture of the seal on page 88.

Buff (tan) and blue are the state's colors. The seal is set in a diamond shape. It reminds us that Delaware's nickname is the "Diamond State" because it is small, but valuable. Another nickname is "the First State" because Delaware was the first state to ratify the U.S. Constitution on December 7, 1787. Can you find the date on the flag?

State Butterfly:
Tiger Swallowtail
The lovely butterfly can be seen in the woods, along streams, rivers, and wooded swamps, and in towns and cities.

State Herb:
Sweet Golden Rod

State Macro-invertebrate:
Stonefly

State Fossil:
Belemnite

LIBERTY AND INDEPENDENCE

DECEMBER 7, 1787

Welcome to Delaware! You live in one of the 50 states of the United States of America. Delaware is the second smallest state in the country.

Delaware's land is great for farming. Most people live in small towns or larger cities. They work to keep Delaware a great place to live.

Delaware in the World

Chapter 1

All of our state's land is close to rivers, bays, or the ocean. Lewes Harbor is along the Atlantic Ocean in the Delaware Bay. Water has played a very important role in our history and is still important today.

geography
grid
hemisphere
latitude
locate
longitude
peninsula

What Is Geography?

Delaware seems very large to us, but it is just one small part of the world. Delaware is our home. It is very important to us. Millions of people all over the world live in places that are important to them.

Geography is the study of how and where people live in the world. When you study geography, you learn about the land, water, plants, animals, and people in different places. They are important to each other.

Where Do You Live?

Most people don't think about it, but geography affects how and where they live. What does this mean?

If your name is Jeff and you live in Delaware, your town or city is on flat or hilly land. It is probably near a river or a stream. The farms out in the country grow vegetables, soybeans, corn, and fruit. The farms get water from the rain. It rains a lot! In the summer, your family goes to the beach. In the winter, you play outside in the snow. You eat potatoes, chicken, spaghetti, and cereal with milk.

The Delaware Adventure

If you are a boy named Sione (see OH nay) and you live on the island of Maui, Hawaii, you have never seen snow float to the ground. You wear flip-flops called "slippers" and shorts to school. You splash in the surf by the palm trees even in the winter. You live on flat or hilly land between high, jagged mountain peaks and the ocean. Water for crops flows down from the mountains in ditches. There is little rain most of the year. Bright green sugarcane and dark green pineapples grow in wide fields between the towns. You eat chicken, Spam®, fruit, and rice many times a week.

As you learn more about geography, you will learn how the land, water, and plants affect how and where people live.

The geography of Delaware and Hawaii is very different, even though both places are next to an ocean. In each place, people have learned to live well.

1 *You know you live on the **planet** Earth, but just where on Earth do you live?*

2 *Continents are huge land areas surrounded by oceans or seas. What **continent** is Delaware part of? Can you name all of the continents?*

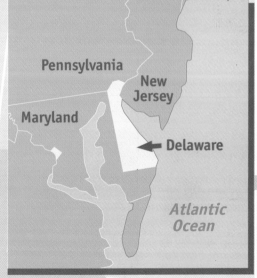

3 *A **country** is a place under the control of a government. What country do you live in? What countries are to the north and south of us?*

4 *Our country has 50 **states**. Delaware is one of the smallest.*

How Do We Locate a Place?

To *locate* means to find. Pretend you meet some new friends who live in another country. How would you tell them where to find you if they come to visit? There are different ways to explain where you live.

You could tell your new friends that our state is next to Maryland and the Delaware River. You could tell them that your town is close to another town or a river.

You can also tell your new friends exactly where you live. Every place on Earth has an exact location. It is the *latitude* and *longitude* of a place.

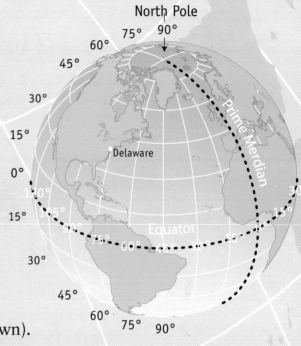

- Latitude lines run east and west (side to side).
- Longitude lines run north and south (up and down).

On a map or a globe, you can see these lines crossing each other to make a *grid.* The places where they cross are an exact location. All along the lines you will find small numbers with tiny circles next to them. Each tiny circle is the symbol for a degree. A degree is part of a circle. The equator is 0 degrees latitude. The prime meridian is 0 degrees longitude. Then the degrees are counted going north or south and east or west.

Don't be fooled, though. The lines are not really on the ground. They are only on maps and globes.

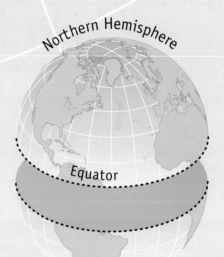

Hemispheres

Look at a globe and find the equator. It is the imaginary line that runs around the middle of Earth like a belt. It neatly divides Earth in two halves, or *hemispheres.* Which hemisphere is Delaware on?

Now find the prime meridian. It is the imaginary line that runs from the North Pole to the South Pole and divides Earth into two different hemispheres. Which one is Delaware on?

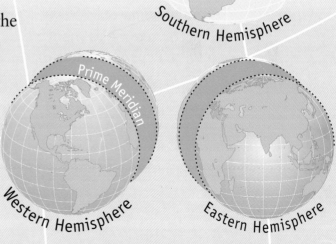

Delaware in the World

The Delmarva Peninsula

A *peninsula* is a large area of land that is surrounded by water on at least three sides. Delaware is part of the Delmarva Peninsula. The name "Delmarva" uses letters from the names of the three states on the peninsula. They are Delaware, Maryland, and Virginia. Can you see how the peninsula got its name?

Do you see the curved boundary line between Pennsylvania and Delaware? Delaware is the only state to have part of a circle as a boundary line. The circle was drawn 12 miles out from the top of the old courthouse in New Castle.

Delaware's shape is kind of like a bowling pin. It is narrow at the top and wide at the bottom.

Activity

Reading a Map

We can learn a lot about places by studying maps. Maps help us know where we are. They help us get where we want to go. What else can you learn from maps?

Use the map on page 9 to answer the questions:

1. What is the title of this map?
2. What symbols are shown on the map?
3. If you wanted to go from Wilmington to Dover, what direction would you go?
4. If you wanted to go from Lewes to Laurel, what direction would you go?
5. About how many miles is it from Claymont to Middletown?
6. About how many miles is it from your town to Dover?
7. Which beaches are closest to 75° longitude?
8. On which latitude line do you find Felton and Frederica?

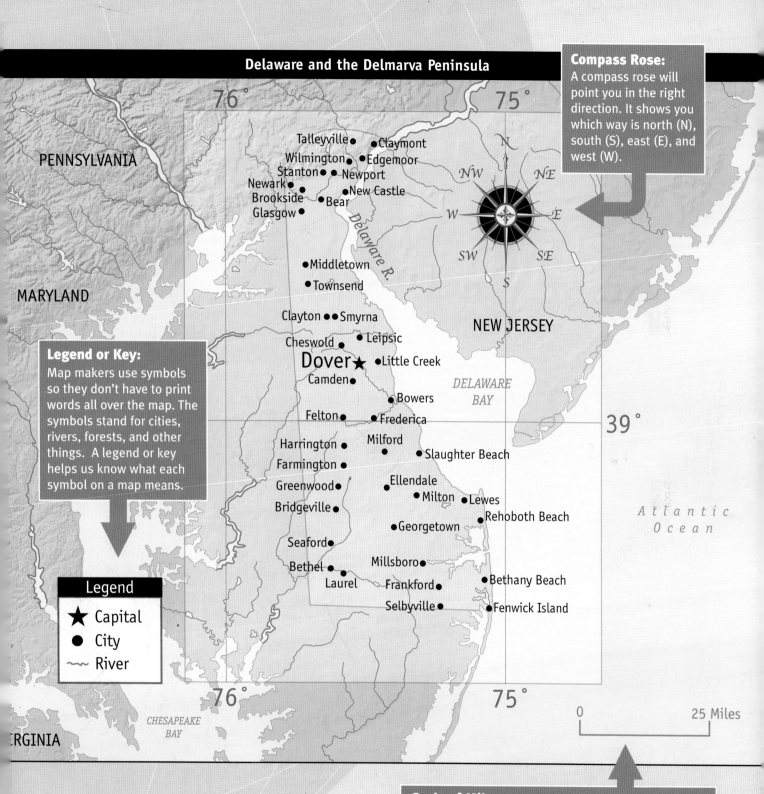

Delaware and the Delmarva Peninsula

Compass Rose: A compass rose will point you in the right direction. It shows you which way is north (N), south (S), east (E), and west (W).

PENNSYLVANIA

76°

75°

Talleyville
Claymont
Wilmington
Edgemoor
Stanton
Newport
Newark
Brookside
New Castle
Bear
Glasgow

Delaware R.

N
NW
NE
W
E
SW
SE
S

MARYLAND

Middletown
Townsend

NEW JERSEY

Clayton • Smyrna
Cheswold
Leipsic
Dover ★
Little Creek
Camden

DELAWARE BAY

Bowers
Felton
Frederica

39°

Harrington
Milford
Farmington
Slaughter Beach

Greenwood
Ellendale
Milton
Bridgeville
Lewes
Rehoboth Beach

Georgetown

Seaford

Bethel
Millsboro
Laurel
Frankford
Bethany Beach
Selbyville
Fenwick Island

Atlantic Ocean

Legend or Key: Map makers use symbols so they don't have to print words all over the map. The symbols stand for cities, rivers, forests, and other things. A legend or key helps us know what each symbol on a map means.

Legend
★ Capital
● City
～ River

76°

75°

CHESAPEAKE BAY

VIRGINIA

0   25 Miles

Scale of Miles: When you are planning a trip, it's good to know how far you will travel. A scale of miles shows how far apart things are. It measures the distance between places.

Water, Water Everywhere

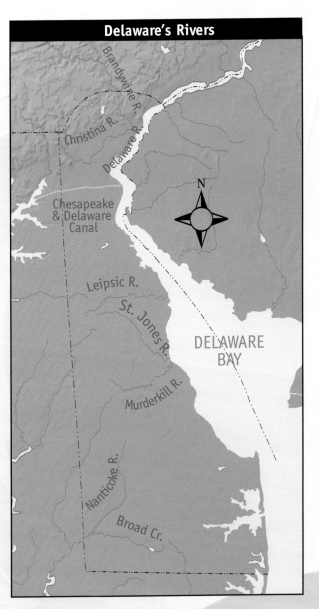

Delaware's Rivers

Brandywine R.

Christina R.

Delaware R.

Chesapeake & Delaware Canal

Leipsic R.

St. Jones R.

Murderkill R.

DELAWARE BAY

N

Nanticoke R.

Broad Cr.

Remember the story of the two boys at the first of this chapter? Both boys have a lot of water all around them! You don't have to travel very far in our state to get to a river, a bay, or the ocean. Besides the large Delaware River, Delaware Bay, and Atlantic Ocean, there are many other rivers, creeks, and ponds.

Fresh Water

Delaware's fresh water includes streams, lakes, and ponds. You may have heard frogs croaking on a summer night. You may have heard the slapping sound of a beaver making its house. You may have spent many happy hours fishing from a boat or a bridge.

Saltwater

Both the Atlantic Ocean and the Delaware Bay are saltwater. Some plants and animals can live in saltwater. Others cannot. Saltwater is home to many sea animals that people like to eat. There are oysters, blue crabs, sea trout, and flounder. The salty ocean is also home to dolphins that you can sometimes see from ocean beaches. People stay away from sharks and jellyfish in the ocean because they can bite or sting!

Water Transportation

People need the Delaware Bay and River for transportation. Ships travel back and forth from ports in Wilmington and Philadelphia. The ships deliver products that are made here. They also bring us things such as cars from Europe, lumber from Canada, and meat and bananas from South America.

That's a Fact!
The Atlantic Ocean:

- is the second largest body of water on the earth. (The Pacific Ocean is larger.)
- touches five continents: Europe, Africa, North America, South America, and Antarctica.
- is 3.5 percent salt. Drinking salty ocean water can make you sick.
- has a floor of mud, covered with shells and millions of tiny dead animals.

High Tide, Low Tide

Tides are affected by the moon. When the moon is full, the high tide is very high and the low tide is very low. Between the full moons, the high tides are not quite as high and the low tides are not quite as low.

1 MEMORY MASTER

1. Describe some ways the lives of Jeff in Delaware and Sione in Hawaii are both different and the same.
2. How can you describe the location of a place?
3. How is water important to the people of Delaware?

environment
humid
pollute
region
rural
suburbs
urban

This lighthouse in Lewes is near Cape Henlopen State Park. At Cape Henlopen, you can visit the Seaside Nature Center and learn about ocean tides, animal life, and ways to enjoy the beach with your family and friends.

Land Regions

Geographers divide land into smaller parts called *regions.* A region has things that are alike in some way. There are farming regions and city regions, where people work in tall office buildings. There are dry desert regions and wet rainy regions. There are mountain regions, hilly regions, valley regions, and coastal regions.

Delaware has two land regions. Most of the state is flat land. This is one region. Our state also has a much smaller region in the north that has high rolling hills. What does the land around you look like?

The Atlantic Coastal Plain Region

Most of Delaware is part of the Atlantic Coastal Plain land region. It is a low, flat land region close to the Atlantic Ocean. The soil of the coastal plain is sandy and has few large rocks. Rivers and streams move slowly in a snakelike pattern across the flat land. Cities and towns have been built next to the many rivers.

Piedmont

Atlantic
Coastal Plain

Down by the Seashore

Delaware's coastline provides wonderful beaches. Cape Henlopen is the place where the Atlantic Ocean meets the Delaware Bay. It is near the town of Lewes. People from all over the country come to enjoy the sandy beaches and the ocean waves. So many people come to Rehoboth Beach from the Washington, D.C., area, that it is sometimes called "the nation's summer capital."

The Wetlands

The wetlands are marshy lands along the coast. The land floods twice a day with saltwater. It mixes with fresh water that runs down in streams. Tall grasses and other plants grow there.

The wetlands are a great place for birds, fish, and other animals. Fish learn to swim in the calm water there before they go out to the ocean.

The Big Cypress Swamp

Swamps are wetlands where many tall trees grow. Bald cypress trees have roots that stick way up out of the water. The trees can grow over 100 feet tall! This is about three times as tall as many other tall trees.

The Atlantic Flyway

Are you a bird watcher? You probably already know that when cold weather is coming, many birds go south to warmer climates. They return in the spring.

The Atlantic flyway is a path that birds take when they fly north and south. Delaware is right under the flyway. The birds often stop in our wetlands to eat, rest, and lay eggs.

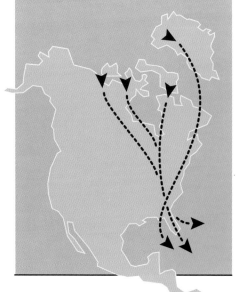

The Piedmont Region

Another land region is a place of rolling hills. The word "piedmont" means "foothills." The hills in this region lead to a mountain range called the Piedmont. It runs through several states and leads to the Appalachian Mountains.

The soil in the Piedmont is filled with stones and rocks. The streams and rivers move swiftly down the hills to the coastal plain below. In a later chapter you will learn how the rivers gave power to move machines in mills and factories.

Most of the land is covered with communities where people live. Only a few farms remain there.

Delaware's largest city, Wilmington, is at the edge of the Piedmont.

The forests in the Piedmont Region are lovely in the fall.

Wilmington is a busy city next to a seaport on the Delaware River. What do you see when you go downtown in the city?

Dover, our state's capital city, is home to our state government. Dover is our second-largest city.

Urban and Rural Regions

All land regions have places where people live and work. Do you live in a city, next to a city, in a small town, or out in the country?

- Cities, or places where a lot of people live, are called *urban* regions.
- Communities next to the cities are called *suburbs.*
- Farmland and places where few people live are *rural* regions. In Delaware, about 40 percent of the land is farmland.

Delaware's Largest Cities and Communities	
City	**Population in 2005**
Wilmington	72,600
Dover	32,000
Newark	28,500
Pike Creek	19,750
Bear	17,600

Delaware in the World

A great place to see a forest is the Brandywine Creek State Park.

In pine forests you will see holly trees with their shiny green leaves and beautiful red berries. The holly is Delaware's state tree.

Amazing Woodlands

Our state has woodlands in both land regions. There are many large forests. Pine trees look beautiful with snow on their branches. Other forests of maple, sycamore, gum, and white oak trees turn beautiful colors and drop their leaves before winter comes. Sunlight shines down through the trees and helps smaller trees, shrubs, vines, and grasses grow. These smaller plants include holly, dogwood, laurel, and a plant you need to be careful of—poison ivy!

Trees provide lumber for homes, furniture, and paper. They give us shade and beauty. Can you imagine a world without trees?

Homes for Animals

Woodlands provide homes for animals. Animals that live in the woods include fox, skunk, opossum, and many kinds of birds and reptiles. In the early evening you can see deer feeding at the edge of a forest. Sometimes they try to cross the road in front of cars, so drivers have to be very careful.

The Delaware Adventure

Preserving Our Environment

Your *environment* is all around you. The land, the water, and the air are part of your environment. Do you live in a dirty or a clean environment? Is it quiet or noisy?

Sometimes things people want can harm their environment. A farmer uses fertilizer to get better crops, but rain may wash the fertilizer into streams and harm the fish. People like to drive cars, but car engines give off gases that *pollute* the air.

How does Delaware protect the environment? Our state government sets aside land that cannot be harmed. No one can build homes or businesses there. Plants and animals are protected.

Our state leaders also make laws that protect the air. Cars are inspected to make sure that they do not give off too much harmful gas. There are laws against polluting the air and the water.

Oil Refineries

Ships on the Delaware River bring oil from South America and Saudi Arabia. The ships carry the oil to large buildings called refineries. In the refineries, the oil is made into gasoline and other oil products. People use the gas for their cars and to heat their homes. One of the largest refineries is near Delaware City.

Sometimes the oil spills into the river. The refineries give off bad fumes. Those spills and fumes can hurt people, animals, birds, and fish.

The government passed a law called the Coastal Zone Act. It says no more factories or refineries can be built along the Delaware coast.

When you visit Bombay Hook National Wildlife Refuge, scan the sky for soaring eagles and osprey. What kinds of birds are in this photograph?

Climate and Weather

To understand a place, you need to know about its climate. Does the place have four seasons—winter, spring, summer, and autumn? Is the place mostly dry or wet? Hot or cold?

Remember Jeff and Sione? They live in places that have very different climates. That means children can play in the snow in one place but not in the other place. It means palm trees can grow in one place but not in the other.

A Mild, Humid Climate

Delaware has a mild climate. It never gets as hot or as cold as some other places in the world. Delaware also has a *humid* climate. Humid climates have no dry season. They get some kind of precipitation every month of the year. There is usually a lot of moisture in the air. On a hot day it can make you feel "sticky" and sweat more.

What can you learn about Delaware's climate and weather by studying this chart of weather words?

Weather Words

Before you can understand weather, you need to know some "weather words." How many of these words do you already know?

- **Precipitation:** rain, snow, sleet, hail that falls to the ground
- **Humidity:** moisture (water) in the air
- **Thunderstorm:** thunder, lightning, and rain
- **Rainstorm:** a heavy downpour of rain
- **Snowstorm:** a strong wind with snow
- **Nor'easter:** a strong windstorm from the northeast that brings rain or snow
- **Tornado:** a fast-turning column of air; a whirlwind
- **Hurricane:** heavy rain and strong winds that start out in the ocean near the equator and rotate counter-clockwise around an "eye"

Delaware's Average Temperatures and Precipitation
Yearly Temperature .....55 degrees
Yearly Precipitation ......45 inches
January Temperature ....34 degrees
July Temperature ....76 degrees

Don't Be Afraid!

Sometimes the weather can be frightening. Delaware often has severe nor'easters. They are storms of strong winds that start in the northeast and move southward. Thunderstorms and snowstorms knock down trees and power lines. The sky gets dark, and the air gets cold.

Tornadoes might pick up cars and roofs and put them down somewhere else. Luckily, Delaware usually gets only about one tornado a year.

Hurricanes can destroy homes and cause floods. They don't usually hit our state, but there have been several bad ones over the years.

② MEMORY MASTER

1. Name and describe Delaware's two land regions.
2. Describe rural and urban communities.
3. What is the difference between climate and weather?

Seawalls help protect the beach from the wind and waves of ocean storms.

CHAPTER ❶ REVIEW

Activity

Mental Maps

Study the shape of our state for a few minutes. Then draw the shape of Delaware from memory. How did you do?

Try it a second time. Is your second map better? Try to add cities to your mental map. Add the Delaware River and Delaware Bay. Can you label the states that touch our borders? Put a mark close to where you live.

Now make a mental map of the United States. Can you add the Rocky Mountains and the Appalachian Mountains? Can you add the Great Lakes? Label the Pacific Ocean, the Atlantic Ocean, and the Gulf of Mexico. Put a star on Delaware.

Activity

The Ways We Use Water

With your classmates, make a list of 20 ways water is used. Your list might include things like drinking, cooking, cleaning, and swimming.

1. Pretend there is not enough water, and you have to take five things off your list. What can you live without? Cross out five uses.
2. How would life be different without each of the things you crossed out?
3. Pretend things just got worse. You must cross off five more uses for water. What are the most important things left on your list?

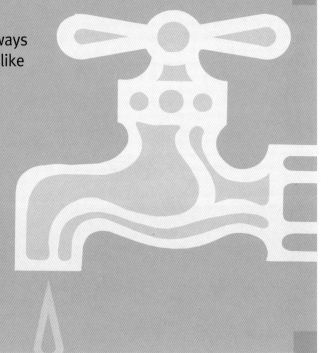

Activity

Where Do Delaware's People Live?

The desks in your classroom are probably spaced evenly in rows or groups. What if you put a lot of desks in one corner of the room and only a few desks in two corners of the room?

People in our state are not evenly spaced on the land. Instead, most of the people live in cities in the northern part of our state where there are many factories, stores, and offices where people work. These places have good roads to other large cities. They have seaports and rivers for water and transportation. Fewer people live far apart from each other on farms or other land out in the country. A few people live by the seashore.

This map shows Delaware's three counties. Use the map to answer these questions: **1.** Which county is the smallest? **2.** Which county is the largest? **3.** Which county has the most people? **4.** Which county has the fewest people? **5.** Why do you think the smallest county has the most people living there?

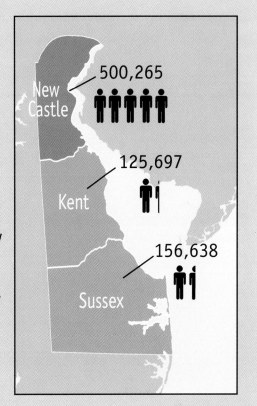

Activity

Compare Climates of the World

Can you find these places on a world map or globe? They all have the same climate as your home. Why?

- Delaware, (state), U.S.A.
- Uruguay (country), South America
- Durban (city), South Africa
- Zhejiang Province, China

The climate of these places is never really, really hot like it is in the country of Saudi Arabia. The climate never gets as cold as Siberia in Russia. Learn more about all of these places and compare their climates to Delaware's climate.

The First People

"You must always help each other and respect the older people.

You must always teach your children to be grateful to their maker."

—A Delaware man

Timeline of Events

| 10,000 B.C. | 9000 B.C. | 8000 B.C. | 7000 B.C. | 6000 B.C. |

8000 B.C.–3000 B.C. —
Archaic Indians live
all over North America.

— 10,000 B.C.–8000 B.C. —
Paleo Indians live
all over North America.

Chapter 2

What did the native people in Delaware look like? How did they live? What tools and weapons did they use to get food? How did groups of people change throughout history?

A.D. 1000
The Lenni Lenape Indians live in villages and begin to farm. Nanticoke Indians hunt here.

5000 B.C.	4000 B.C.	3000 B.C.	2000 B.C.	1000 B.C.	0	A.D. 1000

3000 B.C.–A.D. 1000
Early Woodland Indians live and hunt in many places, including the land that is now Delaware.

23

Paleo Indians

Spear points from 10,000 B.C.

One of the best places to get stone in Delaware was Iron Hill. Ancient people cut the stone and used it to make tools.

• Iron Hill

• Middletown

People first came to North America many thousands of years ago. The Ice Age was ending. The land was still very cold and wet. The people came to hunt huge animals that roamed the land. The people hunted the animals for food. They used the animal skins for clothing. The animals had heavy fur coats that kept the people warm.

The people had to follow the animals to hunt them. This means families moved around all the time. They were *nomads.*

The people needed tools and weapons. They carved sharp spear points from stone and animal bones. They attached the spear points onto long sticks to make a spears. On a hunt, they jabbed the spear into an animal. Many men attacked the same animal, and everyone shared the meat and the fur.

These first people who lived here are called Paleo Indians. Paleo means ancient, or very, very old.

Mastodons and Mammoths

At the end of the Ice Age, herds of very large animals lived on the land.

Mastodons were like giant elephants. Mammoths were even larger. Some of them had long, shaggy fur.

Thousands of years after the giant animals lived here, part of a mastodon tooth was dug up near Middletown. So far, no whole bones of the giant animals have been found in Delaware. They have been found in many other states and in other parts of the world.

A hunter waits with his spear and atlatl.

These stone ax heads were found in Delaware. Archaic Indians used them over 8,000 years ago. Can you see where the ax heads used to be laced onto a wooden handle? What do you think the axes were used for?

Archaic Indians

Over thousands of years, the weather got warmer. The ice melted. The levels of the Atlantic Ocean, the Delaware River, and other rivers rose. More trees and plants could grow in the warmer climate, but the huge animals could not. They became *extinct*. They disappeared from the earth forever.

Smaller animals such as deer, elk, bears, and turkeys roamed through forests, meadows, and marshlands. Many birds flew in the air and made nests in the trees and grasses.

As the climate changed, the people also had to change. The people who lived at this time are called Archaic Indians. Archaic is a word that describes a time when people were figuring out how to make better tools and learning better ways of doing things.

The Archaic Indians made better tools and weapons than the Paleo Indians had made. Men used an *atlatl* (at LATL) to throw spears straighter and faster. They wove nets to catch fish.

An atlatl helped hunters kill faster animals such as deer and elk.

People used a heavy stone to crush nuts, seeds, and grain against a larger stone.

The men used nets and also threw a *bola* to catch large marsh birds such as ducks and geese. They made a bola by tying three stones onto the ends of three long cords. The cords were made of animal *sinew.* Sinew is strips of muscle tendons the people got from the animals they killed.

Hunter-Gatherers

The people were *hunter-gatherers* who hunted wild animals, caught fish in rivers and streams, and gathered wild seeds, nuts, and roots. The women crushed seeds and nuts with heavy grinding stones. They cooked the ground meal in stone pots over campfires.

The women made clothes from animal skins. They sewed the animal skins together with needles made of animal bone and thread made of sinew.

Families on the Move

The people lived in small family groups. The families moved often in search of food. Summer, winter, spring, and fall came and went. The people learned where the animals went during different seasons of the year. They knew where to find seeds, nuts, and roots in different seasons.

At certain times each year the men, women, and children moved from their village to campsites. They followed the same route they had followed the year before.

Hunter-gatherers had to know which plants they could eat and which would harm them.

① MEMORY MASTER

1. What do we call the first people who came to Delaware?
2. What kinds of animals did the Paleo Indians hunt?
3. Why are Archaic Indians called hunter-gatherers?
4. What new tools did the Archaic Indians make?

The Delaware Adventure

Native Cultures

For thousands of years, the *native* people throughout North America still traveled to hunt, fish, and gather food from wild plants. They also began to plant crops and to build bigger villages. The groups who lived together became larger. Groups visited and traded with other people who lived far away.

Each large group shared its own *culture.* Culture means how people live. The land, weather, soil, plants, and animals were not the same across North America. In some places there was plenty of rain. In other places it hardly ever rained and the land was very dry. Some people lived near the ocean where there were crabs and oysters to eat. Other families lived near the mountains where there were plenty of forests and deer.

WORDS TO UNDERSTAND

adobe
culture
native

People in different parts of North America built different kinds of homes and ate different kinds of food. They learned different skills. They had different ideas.

North American Indian Groups

Anasazi

Mound Builders

Eastern Woodland

Anasazi Indians

The Anasazi Indians lived in what is now the south-western United States. The weather was hot and dry most of the year. Most of the rain fell onto the high mountains and plateaus.

The people built large apartment-style homes with hundreds of rooms for many families. In some places they built cliff dwellings where families lived in small apartments attached to one another.

They made the homes of stone or *adobe.* Adobe is heavy clay mixed with straw. It is put into a mold and dried in the sun to make bricks. The bricks are very strong. They last for a very long time.

The Anasazi farmed corn, beans, and even cotton. They raised dogs and turkeys. The people are best known for the baskets and pottery they made.

The people made clay pottery and painted it with bold designs.

The Anasazi built this ancient cliff house in Arizona. Today it is known as the White House Ruins.

Photo by Kindra Klinef

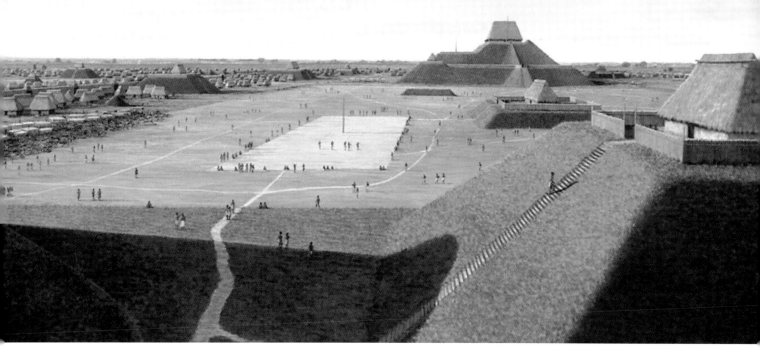

This painting shows Cahokia—City of the Sun. It was built by Mound Builders. What are the people doing? What are their homes and pyramids made from? Why were the taller pyramids built?

Mound Builders

The Mound Builders lived in a huge land region around the Mississippi River and all the way to the Appalachian Mountains. Different groups of Mound Builders built thousands of villages along the rivers. They farmed corn, beans, and squash. They made tools and jewelry. They traded with other native people in faraway places.

The mounds were high piles of earth and stone that look like hills today. Some of the very large hills were shaped like animals such as a snake, turtle, or bird. Others were in the shape of circles or squares. Sometimes an important ruler lived in a home on top of a very high mound. Many of the mounds were places where the people buried their dead.

It could take over 100 years to build a huge mound because the people had to move the dirt in baskets. Load after load, the dirt had to be dug up and carried to the mound.

The people built their homes around the mounds. They used wood, reeds, and grasses for the walls and the roofs. Villages often had large, flat fields where people could buy and sell things they made, meet with friends, or play games.

Woodland children helped guard the crops. They scared away birds that came to eat the corn.

Eastern Woodland Indians

East of the Allegheny Mountains lived many groups of Eastern Woodland Indians. Each group lived on its own, but the groups shared a common culture. That means they all lived in about the same way. The American Indians in Delaware were part of this Eastern Woodland culture.

The people made pottery from clay and baked it until it was hard and strong. They made pottery bowls, cooking pots, and jars. They stored food in the jars so water and insects could not destroy it. The people were good hunters, gatherers, and farmers. You will learn more about them in the next lesson.

Woodland women made pots with long coils of clay. The pots were then baked in a very hot fire until the clay became hard and waterproof.

2 MEMORY MASTER

1. What are the Anasazi most famous for?
2. What are the Mound Builders most famous for?
3. The Indians who lived in Delaware were part of what group?

Back in Time

Close your eyes and pretend to go back in time. Go back hundreds of years when thousands and thousands of American Indians lived in North America. Many of them lived where you live now.

All around you are green forests. See the gentle deer walking among the trees. See the striped chipmunks running on the ground. Can you see thin lines of grey smoke rising above the trees? If you follow the smoke you will see dark-haired boys and girls your age gathering firewood or playing with each other. You might see a small yellow dog running around.

Leave the forest and walk along the beach. Feel the sand on your feet. Can you hear the waves? Can you smell the saltwater? Now find men working hard, pulling fish from nets. Do you wish you could join the people when they go back to their wigwams and eat a hot fish dinner?

Who are these people? How is their life the same as yours? How is it different?

Long ago, native people lived in wigwams. They speared fish in the rivers near their homes.

The First People

31

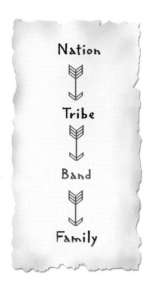

Nation
↓
Tribe
↓
Band
↓
Family

The Indians of Delaware

Two large groups of Woodland Indians lived in today's Delaware. They were the Lenni Lenape and the Nanticoke (NAN-tuh-coke).

• The name Lenni Lenape means "common people" in the Lenape language. Sometimes we just call them the Lenape.
• The name Nanticoke means "tidewater people" in the Nanticoke language.

The Lenape built their homes along the streams and rivers that flowed into the Delaware River. The Nanticoke lived south of the Lenape. They lived along the Nanticoke River between the Delaware Bay and the Chesapeake Bay.

Which man is dressed for winter? Which man is dressed for summer? How do you think the clothes were made? What were they made of?

Lenni Lenape Bands

The Lenape lived in villages made up of family groups called **bands.** Each band was part of a larger group called a **tribe.** Some tribes joined together into **nations.** The Lenape tribe lived in many places. They lived in today's Delaware, New Jersey, and parts of Pennsylvania and New York.

The many Lenape bands shared about the same language, religion, and customs. They were usually peaceful people who did not make war on each other or on other tribes.

What Did They Look Like?

Both men and women painted and tattooed themselves with colored dyes. They wore jewelry made from seashells.

In warm weather men wore aprons and women wore skirts made from deerskins. In cold weather the people wore cloaks made from the fur of deer and bear. They also wore warm leggings and *moccasins.* The people decorated their clothing with shells, beads, feathers, and paint.

More than one family lived in a longhouse.

Homes

The Lenni Lenape lived in wigwams and longhouses. They used thin young trees, large pieces of tree bark, and long grasses to make the homes. Around the inside of the homes the people built wooden platforms to sit and sleep on. They covered the platforms with grass mats or animal skins to make them soft and comfortable. They stored food and tools under the platforms.

A longhouse was built about the same as a wigwam, but it was much larger. Only one family lived in a small wigwam. If you lived in a longhouse, however, some of your grandparents, aunts, uncles, and cousins might live in the same house with you. They would have their own part of the house and their own cooking fires. In your wigwam or longhouse, the smoke is supposed to escape through a hole in the roof, but it still gets very smoky inside. Most of the time you and your parents live, work, and play outdoors.

A wigwam gave shelter to one family.

Inside a longhouse the people hung corn cobs, tobacco, and herbs to dry. After a hunt, even small animals might be hung up out of the way. Can you find the goose being hung from the top of the longhouse?

The Lenape believed that deer and bears were the greatest of all the animals. They called the bear "our grandfather."

Food for All

Hunting and Gathering

The Lenape made bows and arrows to kill deer, bears, squirrels, turkeys, and other animals. They made nets and hooks to catch fish. They also picked up crabs and oysters along the seashore.

If you were a Lenape boy or girl, you would spend a long time in the summer picking fruits and berries from bushes and vines. Don't get scratched by the thorns!

In the fall, when the weather gets cooler and leaves begin to turn bright yellow, orange, and red, your mother asks you to gather acorns, chestnuts, and walnuts in the forests. You and your friends also try to see who can find the most *edible* roots to dig from wild plants in the meadows.

After the work is done, it is time to eat. Your favorite foods are cornmeal mush with maple syrup, roasted deer meat, fish, oysters, and berries. For a special treat, you love beaver tail cooked in bear fat.

Farming

The people hunted animals and gathered wild seeds. They also grew some of their food. Before they could plant their crops, they cleared the land by burning trees or cutting off a wide ring of bark so the tree would die. Then the dead tree was cut down.

The women were usually in charge of farming. They grew corn, beans, squash, gourds, and sunflowers. After the harvest, the food could be eaten fresh or dried and stored for winter.

The people also grew tobacco. They dried the tobacco leaves and carried some in little bags they wore around their necks. The tobacco was supposed to bring good luck. The adults smoked tobacco in pipes during special ceremonies. Because the people smoked tobacco so rarely, it did not cause the health problems that smoking does today.

The first step to planting was to clear away the trees.

Tools

The Lenni Lenape made tools from stone, bone, shell, reeds, and trees. They sharpened stones to make arrowheads, scrapers, and ax heads. They made other tools such as needles and hooks from the bones of animals and fish.

The men made strong wooden ax handles and hoes for farm work. They also used wood and reeds to make parts of weapons such as bows and arrows.

Bows and Arrows

No one knows who first had the idea to build a strong wooden bow that would shoot sharp arrows. Before the bow and arrow were invented, men killed animals by throwing a spear. The bow and arrow made hunting easier because people could shoot arrows faster from a much greater distance.

Traveling

On the ground, the people walked on dirt paths. They carried or pulled whatever they wanted to take with them. Walking was slow.

Traveling by boat was often the fastest and easiest way to get from one place to another. Water moved much faster than people could walk! Before they could travel on the water, the people needed boats. How did they make boats?

Delaware's native people made dugout canoes from chestnut, tulip, or oak trees. First they cut down a large tree. They cut off the branches and saved the thick trunk for a canoe. They put hot coals in the center of the log and let them burn. Then they scraped out the burned wood. They repeated the burning and scraping many times until the log was hollowed out.

3 MEMORY MASTER

1. What was the largest tribe of Native Americans in Delaware?
2. Describe the two kinds of homes the people built.
3. How did the people get food?
4. How did they make clothes?

The Nanticoke

The Nanticoke were a smaller tribe than the Lenni Lenape. They lived about the same way. At first, the Nanticoke hunted in today's Delaware, but they did not live here. They lived on what is now Maryland's Eastern Shore.

Then men came to North America from Europe in wooden sailing ships. Some wanted to stay in America, and they needed land. The Europeans began to push the Nanticokes off their land. Some Nanticoke bands came to Delaware and lived south of the Lenape in the forests and along the rivers.

Food, Homes, and Clothes

Like the Lenape, the Nanticoke people became farmers. They also hunted and fished and gathered wild berries, fruits, roots, nuts, and seeds. They lived in wigwams and made their own tools, clay pots, and clothing.

What Did They Look Like?

People in different cultures usually look different from each other. Nanticoke men sometimes wore a headband with a feather or two in it. They painted their faces with different colors and designs for different occasions. The men often wore tattoos of animals.

Both men and women wore their hair in long braids. Both men and women wore earrings.

Nanticoke women wore knee-length skirts, and the men wore breechcloths with leather pant legs tied on. Neither women nor men had to wear shirts, but they wore deerskin capes when the weather was cool.

PEOPLE TO KNOW

Lydia Clark

PLACES TO LOCATE

Europe
North America
Maryland
Sussex County

WORDS TO UNDERSTAND

cradleboard
wampum

Linking the Past to the Present

Today, the Nanticoke Tribe in Delaware live just like other Americans in towns and on farms. The children go to school and the adults work and take care of their families.

The First People

Mothers and Babies

Nanticoke mothers, like many Native Americans, carried their small babies on *cradleboards.* They placed the baby on the cradleboard that was lined with soft animal skins. They laced the baby firmly on the board. Then they carried the cradleboard around on their backs. The mother could talk to the baby while she worked. The movement of the mother lulled the babies to sleep.

Sometimes a mother set the cradleboard up against a tree. She could work faster, and the baby could look around and watch older children playing or working. As babies grew up, older children or grandparents often took care of them while their mothers worked in the garden.

Children at Work and Play

When they were old enough, the children learned to work with their parents. Indian children had more chores and less time to play than modern children do. But they did have dolls and toys, such as small bows and arrows. They liked to run and play with their friends. They liked to listen to stories, watch animals, wade in streams, and play games.

Tools and Weapons

Hunters used bows and arrows. If they had to go to war, the men fought with heavy wooden war clubs. They sometimes poisoned their enemies. If you had an enemy within your own tribe, you had better test your food before eating it!

Mothers carried their babies on wooden cradleboards. The babies rarely cried because they were wrapped snuggly and rocked gently as their mothers moved.

The Delaware Adventure

Wampum

Nanticokes were known for their beautiful beadwork, or **wampum.** Wampum was used to decorate clothing, as money, and as a symbol of trust.

Like other American Indian tribes, including the Lenape, the Nanticoke people made small white and purple beads from certain kinds of shiny sea shells. They drilled small holes into the beads. Then they strung the beads on long strands of sinew about 6 feet long. Strands of beads were worked into bands from one to five inches wide. The people wore the bands on their wrist, waist, or over their shoulder.

Sometimes shells were woven into designs and patterns that told a story. A person held a wampum belt to show that what he or she was saying was the truth. Wampum was also used like money for trading. Strings of purple beads were worth more money than white beads.

Wampum Shells

Wampum Belt

The Last Speaker of the Nanticoke Language

Lydia Clark was born about 1781 in Sussex County. Her parents were farmers. They were also Nanticoke Indians. They named their daughter Nau-Gwa-Ok-Wa in their native language.

Lydia Clark was proud to be a Nanticoke. She dressed in Indian clothes all of her life. She could also speak the Nanticoke language when she died in 1856.

You can find a marker to Lydia Clark, the last speaker of the Nanticoke language, in the town of Oak Orchard.

A Spiritual People

The people believed that everything, including the sun, moon, and stars, was filled with spirit. Spirits also filled all the things on earth such as fire, water, trees, animals, birds, insects, and stones. The people asked the spirits to help them have a good hunt or to make sick people well. They also believed that some plants could help cure the sick.

Vision Quest

When a boy was 12 or 13 years old, he went on a journey called a vision quest. This was how he found his own guardian spirit. The boy went out alone to the mountains or forest. He went without food or water. When he was scared and hungry, he prayed for his guardian spirit to come and protect him. The spirit might appear as an eagle, wolf, beetle, or some other part of nature. From then on, the boy's guardian spirit would guide him and protect him in times of illness, danger, or distress.

④ MEMORY MASTER

1. What tribe moved into Delaware from Maryland?
2. Describe how the men and women looked.
3. What was wampum? How was it used?
4. What was a vision quest?

How Do We Know?

The early people did not leave written journals or stories to tell us how they lived. However, when they moved or died, they left things behind. They didn't know that these things would be clues called *artifacts*. The artifacts help us learn about people of the past.

Archaeology is the science of studying people of the past. Archaeologists dig carefully into the ground or search in caves to find clues. They look for old tools, weapons, pottery, bones, fire pits, burial sites, and even trash pits.

Millsboro

ancestors
archaeology
artifact
legend
powwow
preserve

What do you think?

What can you learn about people by looking at artifacts? Could there be a problem with saying how people used certain things hundreds of years ago?

What can this dried corn and grinding stone tell us about how native people lived?

Archaeologists carefully dig for clues to the past.

The First People

41

Legends

We can also learn about the lives of Native Americans from *legends.* Legends are stories told out loud from memory. Legends were usually told during the winter when the sun set early in the evening and people stayed indoors around a warm fire.

Older people told the stories to the children. Stories were passed down from one generation to the next, all the way to today.

American Indians told legends that explained how the earth and people came to be. Legends also answered questions about nature, such as why the owl stays up at night or why the fox is so sly. Legends told of animals and spirits coming to teach or help the people. Animals were often used to teach children about how to be strong and good.

A Creation Legend

An old man taught the children that the earth was once covered by water. The man then drew on the ground a picture of a turtle. He said that a giant turtle lived under the water. When it raised its back, the back became the land. A tree then grew on the turtle's back. Animals and people came from the tree's roots. That is how the earth came to be.

Preserving a Way of Life

Over 2,000 American Indians live in Delaware today. Some of these people have not lived in Delaware very long. Others have *ancestors,* or great-great-grandparents, who were Lenni Lenape or Nanticoke. Sometimes today's Indians have parents or grandparents of two or more different tribes and races.

Today's American Indians are proud of their history and culture. They work to *preserve,* or keep, their culture and share it with others. They learn the old ways of making things such as tools and baskets. They talk to older people. They collect stories and legends and then write them down.

Nearly half of the Indians living in Delaware today are part of the Nanticoke Tribe. To help them preserve their past, they have built a Nanticoke Indian Center and a Nanticoke Museum near Millsboro. The Nanticokes have also worked with the state government to protect important Indian sites.

Each September the Nanticokes sponsor a *powwow* in Millsboro. The powwow is a day for sharing Native American culture through singing and dancing. The powwow begins with a grand entry, or line of dancers. The Nanticoke powwow is a colorful, exciting event. Would you like to dance at a powwow?

Dances come from the spirit and music of the ancestors. The graceful steps and colorful clothes at this Nanticoke powwow keep native traditions alive.

Millsboro ●

⑤ MEMORY MASTER

1. What is an artifact?
2. How do archaeologists help us learn about people who lived long ago?
3. What is a legend?
4. How do Native Americans preserve their culture today?

CHAPTER **2** REVIEW

From There to Here

Native Americans were the first people to live in the land we call Delaware. The earliest people were hunter-gatherers. Later Indians also grew crops to provide food. They got material to make their tools, clothes, and homes from wood, stone, clay, plants, and animals.

Native Americans still live in Delaware. They work to preserve the traditions, legends, and crafts of their culture.

What Do You Remember?

With a small group, read the questions aloud and help each other remember the answers. If no one knows an answer, find it in the chapter.

1. What do we call the earliest people who lived in North America?
2. Why did Indians in different parts of North America develop different cultures?
3. On a map, show where the Eastern Woodland Indians, the Anasazi, and the Mound Builders lived.
4. What were the two main tribes of American Indians who lived in Delaware?
5. How did the Lenni Lenape get food?
6. Where did the Nanticokes move from?
7. How can we learn about people who lived long ago?

Geography 🌍 Tie-In

1. On a map, locate the Delaware River, Delaware Bay, Nanticoke River, and the Chesapeake Bay.
2. List three ways that rivers, bays, and the ocean were important to the Indian people.
3. List three ways that rivers, bays, and the ocean are important to us today.

Technology Tie-In

Technology is the tools, skills, and knowledge that people use to meet the needs of life.

1. What tools did the Archaic Indians use when they hunted?
2. What tools did the Lenni Lenape use?
3. What tools did the American Indians probably use to build a wigwam?

Activity

Indian Place Names

Some places in Delaware have Native American names. Here are some of the names. Find them on a map of Delaware.

Appoquinimink River   Mispillon River   Nanticoke River
Assawoman River   Naaman's Creek

Activity

Just for Fun—Indian Games

Your class can play a game that many American Indians played. Divide into groups of six. Each group will need one small wicker basket and six clean peach pits or large nuts in the shell. Each peach pit or nut needs to be marked on one side with the letter "A."

Put the six pits in a basket and give the basket to the first player. The first player tosses the pits into the air (but not too high) and catches as many as he or she can in the basket. Count the number of pits with the "A" side up. Each "A" scores one point.

Pass the basket to the next player and repeat the toss. Keep passing the basket to each player, then go around again. All six students in the group get 10 tosses. The student with the highest score wins.

THE TIME
1480–1768

"I have two plantations which I have bought, and on them alone I live and move about, sowing all kinds of seed during the year. Also I have livestock for the needs of the people of my house, and I live . . . in a manner that I and mine suffer no wants."

—Carl Springer, 1693

Timeline of Events

1492
Christopher Columbus reaches the New World.

1565
The Spanish build the first permanent settlement in the New World.

1480   1500   1520   1540   1560   1580

1497
Amerigo Vespucci explores the coast of South America.

Explorers and Settlers from Europe

In 1683, the first Swedish settlers arrived to begin a colony they called New Sweden.

1607
Jamestown is started.

1638
The Swedes build Fort Christina.
Peter Minuit is lost at sea.

1609
Henry Hudson explores the east coast.

1639
Black Anthony arrives in Delaware.

1664
The English defeat the Dutch and take control.

1704
Delaware gets an Assembly.

| 1600 | 1620 | 1640 | 1660 | 1680 | 1700 | 1720 | 1740 | 1760 |

1618–1620
The first African slaves arrive in the colonies.

1655
The Swedes surrender to the Dutch.

1681
William Penn gets the colony of Delaware.

1768
The Mason-Dixon survey sets Delaware's boundary with Maryland.

1632
David DeVries finds that Zwaanendael has been burned.

1620
Pilgrims start Plymouth colony in Massachusetts.

1631
Zwaanendael is the first Dutch settlement in Delaware.

PEOPLE TO KNOW

Christopher Columbus
Henry Hudson

PLACES TO LOCATE

Africa
Asia
East Indies
Europe
North America
South America
England
France
Holland (the Netherlands)
Italy
Mexico
Spain
West Indies
Atlantic Ocean
Pacific Ocean

WORDS TO UNDERSTAND

conquer
convert
mutiny

The people who live in Europe are called Europeans.

Where Are They?

If you look at a map of the world and find North America, you will see that Europe is the continent across the Atlantic Ocean. You will see that Europe is attached to another continent called Asia.

Now find these countries in Europe: England, Ireland, Scotland, Spain, the Netherlands, Sweden, and Finland. If you can picture the location of these countries in your mind, it will help you understand our early history.

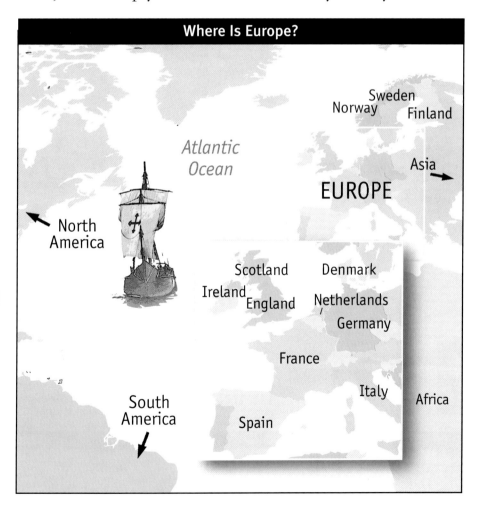

Where Is Europe?

Trading in Faraway Places

The Europeans traded with people in Asia and Africa. Some traders traveled across land. Bad roads, high mountains, and wide rivers made land travel very slow, hard, and dangerous. Robbers sometimes hid behind large rocks or bends in the road and rushed toward the traders. They killed the traders and stole their goods.

Some traders traveled by sea. They built wooden ships that were powered by the wind blowing against sails. They used a compass to help guide the ships at sea.

European sailors began sailing farther and farther away from their home countries. They went to search for gold, jewels, and spices from plants such as nutmeg, ginger, and cinnamon. The spices came from islands near Asia called the East Indies. You can see the East Indies on the map on the next page.

Christopher Columbus

People once believed that the earth was flat. Then they learned more about science. They studied the stars and the sun. They thought the earth must be round. Christopher Columbus, a sailor from Italy, agreed with this view. He was sure that by sailing west across the Atlantic Ocean he could go all around the world and get to the East Indies.

For many years Columbus tried to get someone to listen to his plan. Finally, the king and queen of Spain agreed to give Columbus three small ships and a crew of sailors. The king and queen wanted Columbus to spread their Catholic religion to the people in Asia and the East Indies. They also wanted to find a faster way to bring riches to their country.

Columbus and his crew sailed into the unknown. After many weeks crossing the ocean, they finally saw land on October 12, 1492. Columbus thought he was in the Indies, so he called the people there "Indians." But he had not found the East Indies. He had found a group of islands in North America. Today we call these islands the West Indies.

Pirates!

It was very risky to sail around Africa to get to the East Indies. Many ships were blown far off course and were lost in storms at sea. Some ships were attacked by pirates. The pirates got close to the other ship and shot at it with cannons. Then they climbed up over the sides of the ship and took over the crew. They forced the crew to give them all the valuable goods.

Christopher Columbus

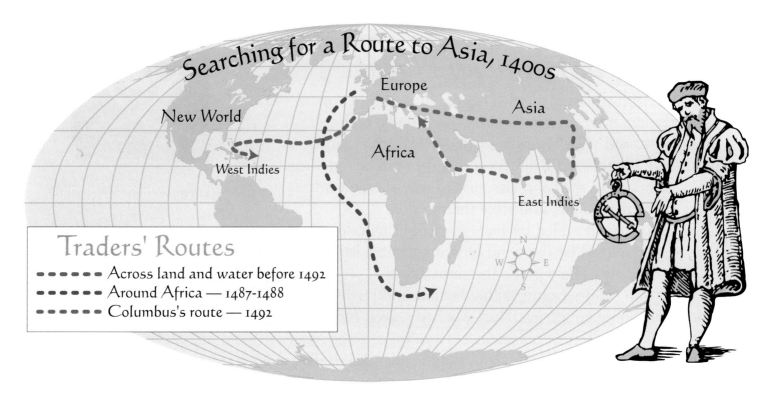

Searching for a Route to Asia, 1400s

New World

West Indies

Europe

Asia

Africa

East Indies

Traders' Routes
- - - - - Across land and water before 1492
- - - - - Around Africa — 1487-1488
- - - - - Columbus's route — 1492

Other Explorers Follow

When Columbus returned to Spain, he told stories of great gold mines and riches on the islands. His stories were not true, but they made kings and queens in other countries want to send explorers to the New World.

Other explorers came from Europe to search for treasure and to claim land in the New World. Men from Italy, Spain, Holland, France, and Portugal explored North America. They claimed land for their countries. They traded with the American Indians.

Spanish explorers searched the New World for gold and other riches. They **conquered** (took over) Mexico and much of South America. They even started the first European town in North America at a place we now call Florida. They named the town Saint Augustine.

Some countries sent Catholic priests to the New World to **convert** the Indians to their religion. To convert means to change. The priests also tried to teach the Indians how to speak, dress, work, and live more like Europeans.

America was named after Amerigo Vespucci, an Italian explorer who came to the New World about five years after Columbus.

Henry Hudson

Over 100 years after Columbus sailed to America from Spain, Holland also wanted to explore the New World. The people who lived in Holland (the Netherlands) are called Dutch. The Dutch also hoped to find a shorter route to the East Indies by sailing west.

The Dutch sent Henry Hudson in a small ship named the *Half Moon* to explore the east coast of North America. He was to search for a river that went all across North America, from the Atlantic Ocean to the Pacific Ocean. They thought this might be a shorter route to China and the East Indies.

Henry Hudson never found the river. Why? Because it does not exist.

Hudson did, however, find the Hudson River and the Delaware River. He met some American Indians who lived along the river. His first mate on the ship wrote in the ship's log book:

Sept. 5 Our men again went on shore and saw a great store of men, women, and children. We went up into the woods and found wild plums. The natives had red copper pipes and things of copper around their necks.

What Happened to Henry Hudson?

Henry Hudson made four trips to North America. He sailed into the Delaware Bay on his third voyage. His fourth trip was a disaster. He sailed far north into the cold waters of Canada. When the water got too icy, Hudson and his crew had to make a camp on land.

When spring came, the starving and angry crew **mutinied.** They accused Hudson of unfairly giving out the small amount of food they had. The sailors put Hudson, his son, and a few other men into a small boat and sent them away. They were never seen again.

1 MEMORY MASTER

1. Where did Europeans travel to buy some of the things they wanted?
2. Why did Christopher Columbus sail west from Spain?
3. What was Henry Hudson looking for when he found the Delaware Bay and the Delaware River?

PEOPLE TO KNOW

David DeVries
James, Duke of York
Lord De La Warr

PLACES TO LOCATE

Massachusetts
Virginia
Jamestown
Zwaanendael

WORDS TO UNDERSTAND

colony
stockade

English Settlements

Jamestown

The English started *colonies* along the coast of North America. A colony is a settlement ruled by another country.

Jamestown was started in today's Virginia. The first colonists were all men. After the first winter, over half of the men had died from cold, disease, and lack of food. Some had been killed by Indians.

The second year, more men and two women came to Jamestown. They farmed and learned how to grow tobacco from the Indians. They sent the dried tobacco leaves to England. In exchange, people in England sold goods such as cloth, metal tools, and tea to the colonists.

Pilgrims

Another group, including 14 children, came to America from England. Why did they come so far to live in a place that had been so hard for the people of Jamestown?

They came to practice their religious beliefs. They did not agree with the official Church of England. At that time, it was against the law not to attend the church.

The people sailed for Virginia. Their ship, the *Mayflower,* rolled up and down in the rough water of the Atlantic Ocean. The little ship ran into icy winds and high waves. Many people got sick during the terrible storms. Finally the ship landed, but it did not land in Virginia. The Pilgrims landed in a place we now call Massachusetts.

The winds grew colder all the time. Snow fell on the deck of the *Mayflower*. For the rest of the winter, the people lived on the ship. The men sometimes left the ship to hunt and explore. They found a place to build a colony in the spring. They would call it Plymouth.

The Delaware Adventure

There was no way to keep the people warm and fed. Once again, about half the people died that first winter.

In the spring, Indians showed the new settlers how to grow corn, beans, and squash. They showed them better ways to fish and hunt. The Pilgrims and the Indians made a promise not to harm each other. They agreed to protect each other from other Indian tribes.

Puritans

The Puritans were another large group from England. Like the Pilgrims, they came to America to practice their religion. The Puritans also settled in Massachusetts. Many Puritans came and started towns. One town became Boston.

Activity

Study a Historic Painting

This painting shows the feast the Pilgrims and Indians shared to celebrate the first harvest. There were no photographs back then, so no one knows exactly what the first Thanksgiving feast looked like. An artist made this painting hundreds of years later.

1. What are the people doing?
2. Do you think an Indian artist would draw the feast in a different way? How might it be different?
3. Do you think the painting shows how the people felt that day?
4. Is the painting a primary or a secondary source?

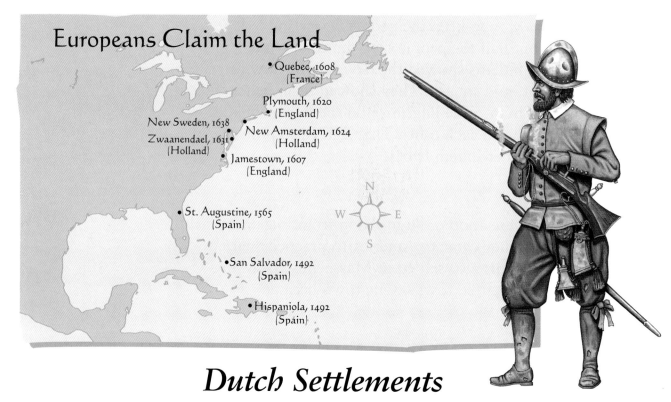

Europeans Claim the Land

Quebec, 1608
(France)

Plymouth, 1620
(England)

New Sweden, 1638

New Amsterdam, 1624
(Holland)

Zwaanendael, 1631
(Holland)

Jamestown, 1607
(England)

St. Augustine, 1565
(Spain)

San Salvador, 1492
(Spain)

Hispaniola, 1492
(Spain)

Dutch Settlements

Do you remember Henry Hudson? The Dutch had sent him to explore North America. He sailed along the coast and found the Hudson River and the Delaware River. He helped the Dutch claim land along the rivers.

The Dutch started colonies in today's New York and New Jersey. They called New York "New Amsterdam" after a city in Holland. They called the other land "New Netherland."

Zwaanendael

The first European settlement in Delaware was Zwaanendael. Zwaanendael means "Valley of the Swans" in Dutch. It was a small settlement of about 30 men from Holland. It was built just inside Cape Henlopen.

The men built a *stockade* around Zwaanendael to protect it. A stockade is a fence made of strong tree trunks. Then they planted crops and started to look for whales in the bay. They wanted to catch whales, drag them onto the beach, cut them up, and then boil them. In this way, they

Zwaanendael •

could get whale oil from the blubber, or fat. Then they could sell the oil to people in Europe. Europeans wanted the whale oil to burn in lamps to make light. They also made candles from whale oil.

Bad Feelings

The Dutch settlers tried to get along with the Indians. Both groups gave one another gifts. But their cultures were very different. Sometimes there were bad feelings.

One day an Indian man ran off with the metal coat of arms that the Dutch had nailed to a pole. The coat of arms was a symbol of Holland, like a flag is today. The Dutch were very angry that their coat of arms had been stolen.

Some Indian men were afraid of the angry Dutchmen. They thought they could make the Dutch happy by killing the Indian who had taken the coat of arms. Other Indians then blamed the Dutch for their friend's death.

One day, while the Dutchmen were working in their cornfield, the angry Indians snuck up on the stockade. A large, growling dog guarded the gate. The Indians began shooting arrows at the dog and killed it.

Once the dog had died, the Indians captured the stockade. Then they went into the field where the Dutchmen were working and killed all of them.

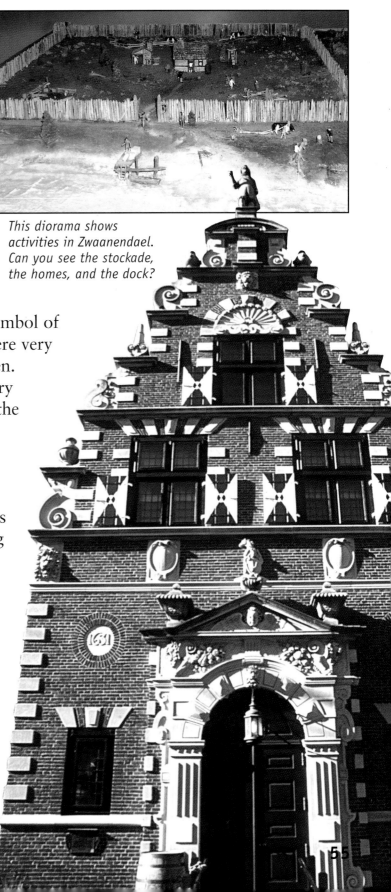

This diorama shows activities in Zwaanendael. Can you see the stockade, the homes, and the dock?

At the Zwaanendael Museum in Lewes you can learn more about the first European settlement in Delaware. The museum was built to look like an old town hall in Holland.

David DeVries found the burned stockade at Zwaanendael.

The Dutch Return

The next year a Dutchman named David DeVries arrived. He found that the stockade at Zwaanendael had been burned. Indians told him what had happened there. DeVries left the stockade and sailed up the bay into the Delaware River.

DeVries was impressed with the land and the river. He wrote in his journal:

> This is a very fine river and the land all beautifully level, full of groves of oak, hickory, ash, and chestnut trees, with many wild grape vines growing upon them. The river has a great plenty of fish—perch, roach, pike, and sturgeon.

Trading for Fur

The Dutch began to trade with the Lenni Lenape Indians who lived along the river. Dutch traders were eager to buy furs for winter coats and hats. They especially liked beaver fur because it was very warm and soft. The traders did not buy the furs with money. They traded for it with glass beads, iron pots, cloth, and sometimes guns and liquor.

The governor of the colony of Virginia was Lord De La Warr.

How Delaware Got Its Name

Delaware got its name from a man who never saw the place. One day, a ship captain from Virginia sailed into a bay to escape a storm. Since the bay did not have a name on his map, the captain decided to call it Delaware Bay in honor of the governor of his colony. The bay, river, Indian tribe, colony, and later, the state, were all called Delaware.

② MEMORY MASTER

1. Tell about the English groups who came to settle North America.
2. Tell about Dutch activities in North America.

A Swedish Colony

The Swedes were the first to create a successful colony in Delaware. Sweden is a country in Europe. The king of Sweden planned the colony to get furs for his company. But the king died before the colony got started.

Queen Christina

The new ruler of Sweden was a six-year-old girl named Queen Christina. She was too young to rule, but men acted in her name to start a colony. They chose Peter Minuit to lead two small ships to North America.

After a long trip across the ocean, the ships landed along the banks of a small river that flows into the Delaware River. The Swedes named the small river Christina in honor of their young queen. They built a fort of logs and dirt in the shape of a star. They called it Fort Christina.

The people called their colony New Sweden. They built a fort and a stockade to protect the colony. They farmed and built log homes. The place where they settled is now part of the city of Wilmington.

The First Log Cabins

Not all of the settlers were Swedes. Many were from Finland, a country close to Sweden. Both Swedes and Finns were used to living in forests. They knew how to build warm houses with logs. These were the first log cabins in America.

PEOPLE TO KNOW

Black Anthony
Christina, Queen of Sweden
Peter Minuit
Johan Printz
Peter Stuyvesant

PLACES TO LOCATE

New York
New Castle
Christina River

WORDS TO UNDERSTAND

surrender

People from Sweden and Finland built log cabins much like this one now at Johan Printz Park in Salem, New Jersey.

Explorers and Settlers from Europe

Johan Printz

The most important governor of New Sweden was Johan Printz. He was very tall and very fat. The Indians called him the "Big Tub." Governor Printz had been an officer in the army. His word was law. Governor Printz made sure that the colony would succeed.

Black Anthony

One member of the New Sweden colony was an African slave. His name was Anthony. The Swedes called him Black Anthony. He was the first person from Africa to live in Delaware.

Johan Printz ruled New Sweden with harsh punishments and made enemies of the Indians and his own people.

A Lost Leader

Peter Minuit was sent to start a colony called New Sweden. He had been to North America before. He had traded with the Indians for some important land. He traded about $24 worth of cloth, beads, and metal pots for some land that is now New York City.

Minuit later led two ships across the Atlantic, again traded with the Indians for land, and helped Swedish settlers build Fort Christina. Then Minuit set sail for Sweden with a load of furs and tobacco. He never made it back. He drowned in a storm.

The Delaware Adventure

The Dutch Attack New Sweden

Peter Stuyvesant was the governor of a Dutch colony called New Netherland. It included today's New Jersey. Stuyvesant had been in wars before and had lost a leg. He was a tough leader.

Governor Stuyvesant wanted to get rid of New Sweden. He wanted the land to belong to the Dutch. He also wanted the furs the Indians were trading to the Swedes.

Stuyvesant built a fort on the Delaware River. He built it just south of the Swedish Fort Christina. When the Swedes captured his fort, Stuyvesant decided to attack New Sweden. He led seven Dutch warships up the Delaware River. When the Swedes saw how powerful the Dutch were, they **surrendered.** The Swedes and Finns stayed on the land and worked on their farms.

The Dutch started a new town on the Delaware River. They called it New Amstel. New Amstel was a harbor where trading ships could dock. Today we call it New Castle.

Stuyvesant had the nickname "Peg Leg Pete" because of his wooden leg.

Wilmington
• (Fort Christina)
• **New Castle**
(New Amstel)

The English Take Over

Only 10 years after the Dutch took over New Sweden, the English went to war with the Dutch. The English captured New Amsterdam and renamed it New York in honor of the Duke of York. He was the brother of the English king. Then the English captured New Amstel and renamed it New Castle. New Castle is still a Delaware town.

3 MEMORY MASTER

1. What did the Swedes do to help settle Delaware?
2. How did the town of New Castle get started?
3. What country ruled after the Dutch?

PEOPLE TO KNOW

King Charles II
Jeremiah Dixon
James, Duke of York
Charles Mason
William Penn

PLACES TO LOCATE

England
Pennsylvania
Lewes
Kent County
New Castle County
Sussex County

WORDS TO UNDERSTAND

dispute
survey

William Penn

William Penn was a rich young man who lived in England. He joined a religious group called the Quakers.

English leaders did not like the Quakers at all. Like the Pilgrims and the Puritans, the Quakers refused to attend the Church of England. The Quakers were beaten and put in jail for their beliefs.

Then William Penn wrote a short book that said the Church of England was against God's true religion. Penn was thrown into jail with other Quakers. "You will die in prison unless you give up these beliefs," the men said.

"Then I'll die in prison," Penn replied. "How can I go against the will of God?"

George Fox was the first Quaker.

The Society of Friends

The real name of Penn's religion was the Society of Friends. The people in the society were called Quakers. Here are some of their beliefs:

• There is part of God in everyone.
• No one was more important than anyone else, so they did not have ministers and they would not bow to a king.
• They called everyone "thee" and "thou."
• They dressed in plain clothes. What was inside a person was most important.
• They would not kill anyone, so they would not go to war. Problems should be resolved by friendly understanding.

A Charter from the King

William's father was a friend of King Charles II of England. He owed William Penn's father a lot of money. When his father died, young William said he did not want the money back. Instead, he wanted land in America. He wanted to create a colony where the Quakers could live in peace.

King Charles gave William Penn the colony of Pennsylvania, which means "Penn's Woods."

The Three Lower Counties

Penn was happy to get Pennsylvania. But he also knew that without the Delaware Bay and the Delaware River, it would be hard for people to come to Pennsylvania. At that time, sailing on the water was much easier than traveling across the very poor dirt trails by horse and wagon.

William Penn received the Pennsylvania Charter from King Charles II.

This charter gave William Penn land that later became Delaware.

James, the Duke of York, was King Charles's brother. James owned the land that Penn wanted. He agreed to give another piece of land, called the "Three Lower Counties on Delaware," to William Penn.

One of the counties was New Castle County. Penn named the two other counties Kent County and Sussex County. The counties were named after places in England.

Dover became an important town in Kent County. Lewes became an important town in Sussex County. These towns were also named after places in England.

Penn Comes to His Colonies in America

Several years later, William Penn, his wife and children, and other Quakers came to America aboard the ship *Welcome*. After the long trip, the ship landed at New Castle.

The people of the town came to meet Penn and his family. They gave Penn three gifts. They gave him the key to the fort, a bowl of river water, and the twig from a tree. These items were symbols of the land and water that now belonged to William Penn.

A General Assembly

William Penn created three other counties in Pennsylvania. Then he asked the people of all six counties to elect their best citizens to help make laws for both of Penn's colonies. The group would be called a General Assembly.

Penn hoped that the people of his two colonies would want to join together into one, but they did not. Why?

- Most of the people who came to Pennsylvania were Quakers. They did not believe in war. They would not vote to buy guns, train soldiers, or build forts.

  - Most of the people in Delaware were not Quakers. They lived close to the ocean and wanted forts and guns to protect them from pirates.

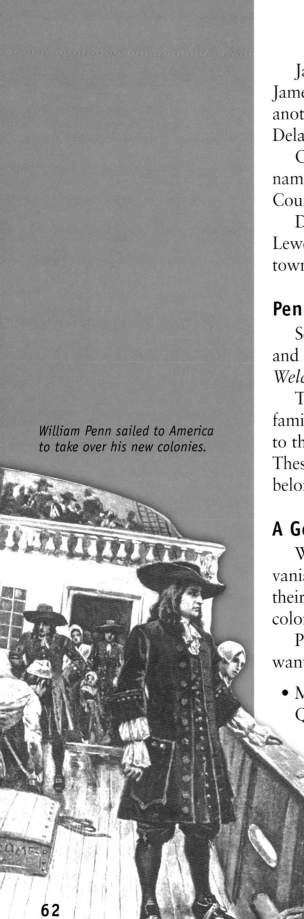

William Penn sailed to America to take over his new colonies.

The Delaware Adventure

After many years, Penn saw that he could not make his two colonies into one. He allowed the people of Pennsylvania and the people of Delaware to elect their own assemblies to make laws. This was an important step toward Delaware later becoming a state.

A Meeting with the Native Americans

Very soon after he arrived, Penn visited the Delaware people. Legend says that Penn met Tamanend, a Delaware chief, under a huge elm tree. Men from the Susquehannock and Shawnee tribes were there, too. Penn told them he planned to live in peace with them. The two groups agreed to trade with each other.

Penn learned the Delaware language so he could speak with them. He went to their feasts and games, and he invited them to his. He signed treaties with them to get more land, instead of just taking it. The Native Americans and colonists lived peacefully together for 50 years.

Pirates on the Delaware

Pirates sometimes raided homes and farms along Delaware Bay. Once 50 pirates attacked Lewes. They stole sheets and blankets, dishes, clothing, guns, and even farm animals.

Another time pirates sailed up the Delaware River as far as New Castle. While people watched from the shore, the pirates stole a ship and sailed away.

Captain Kidd and Blackbeard are famous pirates who sailed in the water around Delaware. Imagine the stories the children must have told about these pirates!

Delaware's Borders

PENNSYLVANIA

NEW JERSEY

MARYLAND

DELAWARE BAY

DELAWARE

You can still find Mason-Dixon markers along our border with Maryland.

Delaware's boundary lines were already set when William Penn got the three counties from the Duke of York. Delaware's boundary with Pennsylvania is a 12-mile arc. An arc is part of a circle. The center of the 12-mile arc is New Castle. Delaware also had two boundaries with the colony of Maryland. The colony's owner, Lord Baltimore, claimed that parts of Delaware belonged to him. William Penn disagreed.

The *dispute* went before a court in England. The court decided in favor of Penn. The court ordered a *survey* of the border lines. A survey is a way of measuring land and drawing boundary lines on a map.

The job of drawing Delaware's borders was very hard. It took two Englishmen to get the lines drawn right. These two men were Charles Mason and Jeremiah Dixon.

Mason-Dixon Markers

First, Charles Mason and Jeremiah Dixon drew Delaware's western borders on a map. Then other men used the map to decide where to put boundary stones on the ground. Every mile they dug holes for a small stone. Every five miles they marked the boundary with a large stone, called a crown stone. It showed the coat of arms of both the Penn family and the ruling family in Maryland. You can still see Mason-Dixon markers along this border today.

④ MEMORY MASTER

1. Who were the Quakers?
2. What two colonies did William Penn rule in America?
3. What did the General Assembly do?
4. Why are Charles Mason and Jeremiah Dixon important?

The Delaware Adventure

Work, Work, Work

Even before William Penn came to America, English settlers were farming in Delaware. Some planters from Maryland also came to Delaware because it had good soil. They grew corn and tobacco.

Most farm families did all the work themselves. Other people could afford to pay workers. Workers helped chop down trees, prepare the ground for planting, plant crops in the spring, and harvest them in the fall. Workers also took care of the horses, cows, chickens, and other farm animals.

Farmers sometimes paid workers to help plant and harvest crops. Farmers also bought slaves to do the work. Slaves were not paid. What are these workers doing?

Explorers and Settlers from Europe

Slavery

A farmer could hire a man and pay him to help with the heavy work. Another way to get help was to buy slaves from Africa. The Africans had been farmers in their own land. They knew how to clear land, plant, and harvest crops.

Slavery has existed from early times and in many places. Slavery existed in all the American colonies. Most slaves lived in the colonies that raised tobacco.

Slavery was a very unfair way to get work done. The Africans who did the work did not get paid. They had no freedom. They were bought and sold. Part of the family could be sold away from the rest of the family.

Most slaves lived in small homes, wore scratchy clothes that did not fit well, and ate cheap, boring food. They were not given nice things no matter how hard they worked. They were not sent to school or taught to read or write.

There were never as many slaves in Delaware as in nearby Maryland and Virginia. The reason was because most Delaware farmers stopped growing tobacco and started growing wheat. Growing wheat took less work than growing tobacco.

Enslaved workers used a hoe to remove weeds.

A heavy iron ball and chain was sometimes locked on the leg of a slave so he or she couldn't escape.

The Delaware Adventure

Indentured Servants

There was another reason why Delaware did not have a large number of African slaves. Farmers often hired servants instead of buying slaves. Most of the servants came from England or Ireland. They were poor people who could not find jobs at home.

Sometimes the servants signed an agreement called an indenture. It said that the servant would work for a period of time, usually for seven years. In exchange, the master would pay for the servant to come to America on a sailing ship. The master would not pay the servant, but would provide clothes, food, and a place to sleep.

The agreement was written on the top of a piece of paper and then again at the bottom. The paper was then cut in half, so that both the master and the servant would have a copy. Since no two cut pieces of paper were exactly the same, only those two pieces of paper would fit together.

During the years of work, the servant was treated much like a slave. The food and clothes were very poor. The men and women were homesick for their families back home.

Then, after years of plowing, planting, harvesting, caring for animals, scrubbing floors, cooking, and washing clothes for other people, the servant was free. Many were then able to work for wages and buy a farm or start a business.

Look at the top of this paper. Why was the paper not cut straight across?

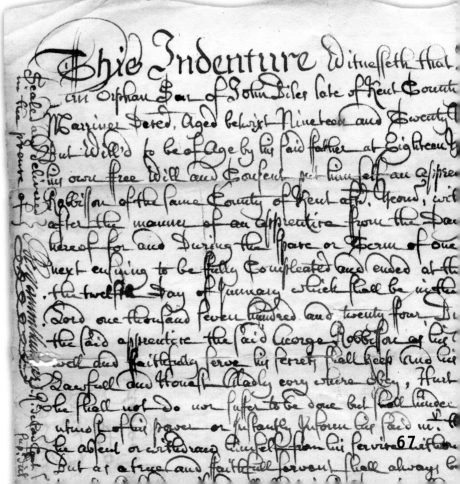

The Dickinson Plantation

I n Kent County, pigs and cattle grazed in the marshlands along the St. Jones River. Forest land provided wood for heating, cooking, and building fences and farm buildings.

Samuel Dickinson owned the most land in Kent County. He divided his land into six farms called *plantations.* Many people worked on his farms. Some were slaves. Others were *tenant farmers* who rented their farms from Dickinson.

At first the slaves and tenant farmers raised tobacco. Then Samuel Dickinson's son John found they could make more money growing grains such as wheat and corn.

You can visit the Dickinson Plantation to see how a wealthy planter lived. You can also see how the white servants and black servants and black slaves lived and worked.

• Dickinson Plantation

These modern people are dressed as Dickinson's servants. How does the slave cabin compare to the house where Dickinson lived?

Dinah

Dinah was one of Samuel Dickinson's slaves. When Samuel died, one of his sons sold Dinah and her daughter. When Samuel's other son, John, found out about the sale, he bought Dinah and her daughter back again. John later freed Dinah and all of his slaves.

Dinah stayed on John's farms for the rest of her life. She was an expert at using a spinning wheel to turn flax and wool into thread. Then she wove the thread into cloth. Each year Dinah made clothes for 10 people.

The Scots-Irish

The Scots-Irish had this double name because they were people from Scotland who had moved to Ireland before coming to America. Many Scots-Irish came to Delaware as indentured servants. Many settled around Newark.

Education

The Scots-Irish thought education was very important. Francis Alison, a minister, started a school for boys. The school became Newark Academy. It prepared young men for college.

The Quakers started a school in Wilmington for both boys and girls. Wilmington Friends School still exists.

Most boys and girls in Delaware, however, had no chance to go to school. There were no free schools, and many parents did not have enough money to pay for private schools. Children learned farming or sewing at home.

The Delaware Colony Grows

The Delaware colony grew. Most of the people who lived in the colony were English, African, or Scots-Irish. Most people lived on farms. A few lived in the small towns of Lewes, Dover, New Castle, or Wilmington.

Men built houses of logs or wooden boards. Wealthy people built brick houses. There were other buildings such as barns, mills, and churches. The largest buildings were churches and government buildings.

Old Swedes Church is the oldest church building in Delaware. It is in Wilmington near the banks of the Christina River.

Triangular Trade

A merchant makes money by buying and selling for other people. Today, a person who runs a store is a merchant. So is a person who ships goods around the world so people can buy them.

William Penn's city of Philadelphia became the largest and most important shipping port on the Delaware River. Ships from Philadelphia sailed to faraway places across the ocean. This pattern of trade is called triangular trade because ships went to three different ports on one journey.

How did it work? *Merchants* from Philadelphia sent ships loaded with barrels of flour to the West Indies. They traded the flour for sugar. Then the ships took the sugar to England. In England they sold the sugar and bought manufactured goods like glass, furniture, and guns to bring back to America. The ships were constantly moving from place to place, carrying goods the people wanted to buy or sell.

A group of Quakers started the city of Wilmington. Many of the men became merchants and sea captains in the triangular trade.

Philadelphia

glass, guns, furniture

Europe

flour

sugar

West Indies

Wilmington

Elizabeth Shipley's Dream

Elizabeth and William Shipley were Quakers who lived in Pennsylvania. William was a merchant. Elizabeth was a leader among the Quakers. One night she had a dream. In her dream she saw a beautiful place where three rivers flowed together. She knew that God wanted her to live there.

Sometime later, Elizabeth rode her horse to Delaware to meet the Quakers there. As she rode, she was surprised to see three rivers before her. They were the Brandywine, the Christina, and the Delaware Rivers.

Elizabeth hurried home to tell her husband what she had seen. William agreed to move to the new town we now call Wilmington. He became a very successful merchant there.

Many other men also became merchants and sea captains in the triangular trade. Wilmington became a busy seaport.

One Boy's Story

Sadly, people who worked with the triangular trade were not always good people. Some kidnapped young boys in Europe and made money by forcing them to work as indentured servants in the colonies.

> I am writing to you to let you know about my coming to this country. . . . I was kidnapped and against my will taken on board an English ship, and ... was brought to ... Virginia. When I arrived there I was sold like a head of cattle to work . . . for five years.
>
> My work was unbearable. It was severe in the summer in the daytime. In the winter my work was . . . to clear land and to cut down the woods and to prepare the soil for the planting of tobacco and Indian corn.
>
> When I faithfully served my time, I heard accidentally that there were Swedes at the Delaware River. . . . I undertook the journey of some 400 miles, and when I arrived there I met the old people and they treated me in a very friendly manner.
>
> —from a letter that Carl Springer wrote to his mother in Sweden

Carl Springer stayed in Delaware and had a very happy and successful life. He married, had a family, bought land, and became a leader in the Old Swedes Lutheran Church.

The 13 colonies used metal coins and printed paper money.

The Role of Money

Today, we use money to pay for the things we need. How did colonists pay for what they needed?

There was little real money used in early Delaware. Instead, most people traded with each other. A farmer might trade eggs and vegetables for shoes. Sometimes colonists paid with tobacco leaves. Sometimes they used English, Spanish, or French coins. They got the coins when they sold things to merchants in faraway places.

Explorers and Settlers from Europe

Mills on the Brandywine

Farmers took their wheat to a large building called a mill. Inside the mill, huge stone wheels ground the wheat into flour. The power that turned the heavy stone wheel came from falling river water. The falling water pounded onto wide slats around a huge wheel and made it turn.

One of the best places to build a mill was on the Brandywine River. The Brandywine mills ground more wheat into flour than any other mills in America. They were called gristmills.

Brandywine flour was part of the triangular trade. The flour was put into wooden barrels. The barrels were loaded on ships that sailed to the West Indies.

There were also mills along other streams in the Delaware Colony. These mills were small. After the harvest, farmers brought their wheat and corn to these mills. The farmers sold some of their ground flour and cornmeal, but they kept most of it for their families to eat.

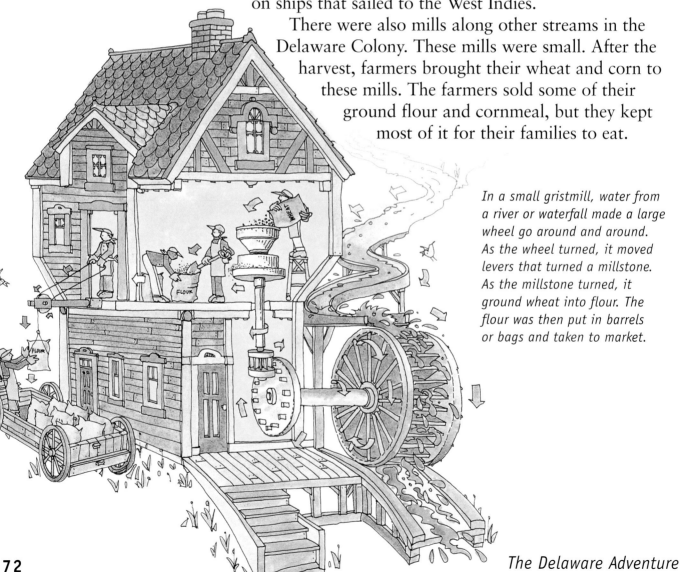

In a small gristmill, water from a river or waterfall made a large wheel go around and around. As the wheel turned, it moved levers that turned a millstone. As the millstone turned, it ground wheat into flour. The flour was then put in barrels or bags and taken to market.

The Delaware Adventure

What Became of the Indians?

After the traders and settlers came from Europe, life for the Delaware Indians changed. Many Indians died from European diseases such as smallpox, chickenpox, and measles.

The settlers wanted to buy the lands that the Indians used for hunting, fishing, and farming. The Indians killed most of the beaver so they could trade beaver fur for other things they wanted. After a while, they had nothing to trade with the settlers. Almost all of the Indians had to move away.

Linking the Past to the Present

Today, most Delaware Indian people live in the state of Oklahoma. Others live in Canada and other places.

A shaman, or medicine man, tried to heal the sick. The Indians got deadly diseases from the settlers. Thousands died.

5 MEMORY MASTER

1. What crops did farmers grow?
2. How were slaves different from servants?
3. What was the triangular trade?
4. What did water-powered mills do?

CHAPTER ③ REVIEW

From There to Here

Europeans from England and Holland explored the east coast of North America. They built settlements there. The Pilgrims came. Then the Puritans came. The Dutch and Swedes started colonies in Delaware. Later, the English took over. King Charles II and his brother, James, the Duke of York, gave land to William Penn.

Delaware became a colony of farms and small towns. The farm workers included African slaves and indentured servants from England, Ireland, and Scotland. Delaware grew.

What Do You Remember?

1. Why was Columbus's voyage important for the world?
2. Why were the Dutch thinking about Delaware?
3. Why were settlements in Delaware located by water?
4. Where did the early settlers of Delaware come from?
5. Why was William Penn important to our state's history?
6. Who did the hard work on farms?
7. How were farms, mills, and trade connected?

Geography 🌍 Tie-In

Find New Sweden, New Castle, Dover, and Wilmington on a map of Delaware. Also find Philadelphia in the state of Pennsylvania. What do all of these sites have in common? Talk about your answer with your class. Does your town or city have something in common with these places?

1. What tools, skills, and knowledge did Columbus and the other explorers use to get from Europe to America?
2. How did the colonists grind wheat and corn into flour or meal? Do you think the American Indians ground their wheat and corn the same way? Why or why not?

Activity

Primary Source—William Penn's Letter

On the left is William Penn's letter to the Indians, in his own handwriting. On the right are the typed words that are easier to read.

To My Friends,

There is one great God and power that hath made the world and all things therein. . . . This great God hath written his law in our hearts, by which we are taught and commanded to love, and help, and do good to one another . . . [I hope to] live together as neighbors and friends and to win and gain your love and friendship, by a kind, just, and peaceable life.

I am your loving friend, William Penn

1. Who wrote the letter, and when?
2. To whom was it written? Why?
3. How does Penn say people should treat each other?

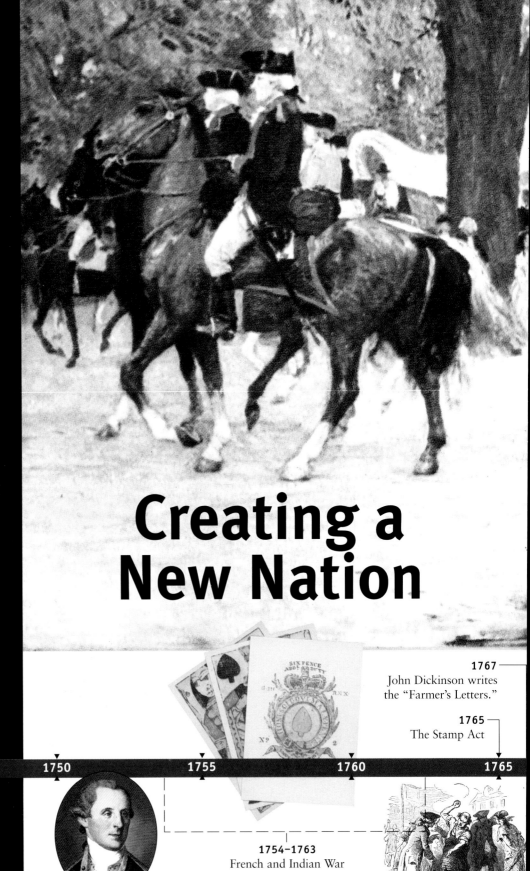

"*That all Government . . . originates from the People . . . and is instituted solely for the Good of the Whole.*

That every member of society hath a right to be protected in the enjoyment of life, liberty and property."

—*Delaware Declaration of Rights, 1776*

Creating a New Nation

1767
John Dickinson writes the "Farmer's Letters."

1765
The Stamp Act

Timeline of Events

| 1750 | 1755 | 1760 | 1765 |

1754–1763
French and Indian War

Soldiers marched to the sound of drums as they left Delaware to join General Washington's army. How do you think the men felt as they marched off to war? How do you think their mothers, wives, and children felt as they saw the men march away?

1775
Battles of Lexington and Concord

1774
The First Continental Congress meets in Philadelphia.

1777
Wilmington is captured by the English.

1781
The English surrender at the Battle of Yorktown.

1787
Delaware becomes the first state to ratify the U.S. Constitution.

1770   **1775**   **1780**   **1785**   **1790**

1773
Boston Tea Party

1776
The Second Continental Congress meets.
• **June 15** Separation Day
• **July 2** Caesar Rodney rides to Philadelphia to vote for independence.
• **July 4** Declaration of Independence is proclaimed.
• **September 21** Delaware writes its first state constitution.

1789
The U.S. Constitution becomes law. George Washington is the first president of the United States.

The Thirteen Colonies

England had 13 colonies in North America. Delaware was one of the smallest colonies. All the thirteen colonies were on the coast of the Atlantic Ocean. Some of the colonies had towns as far west as the Appalachian Mountains. A few, including Pennsylvania, claimed land beyond the mountains.

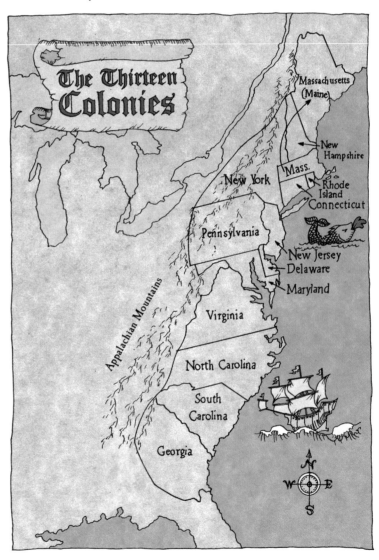

The Thirteen Colonies

Find Delaware on the map. Our state was one of the 13 colonies ruled by England. Was Delaware larger or smaller than the other colonies?

The Delaware Adventure

Who Owned the Land?

American Indian tribes lived west of the Appalachian Mountains. The people in some of the colonies wanted to move onto that land to start farms and towns.

France also claimed the land. Frenchmen had explored the vast area of the Mississippi River and the Great Lakes. The French had also created a colony called Canada north of the English colonies. The Indians liked the French because the French did not plan to settle on Indian lands. They just wanted to trade with the Indians for fur.

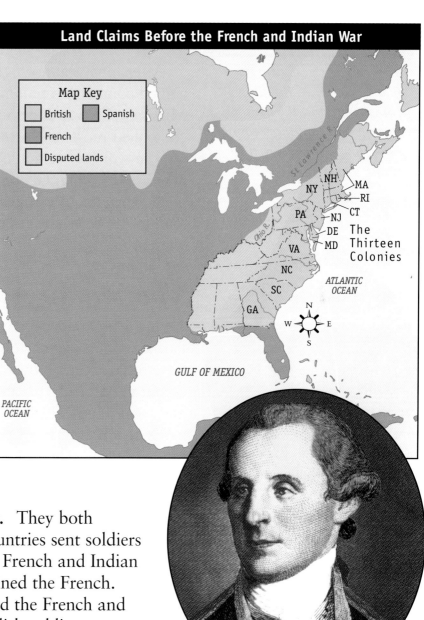

Land Claims Before the French and Indian War

Map Key
British
French
Spanish
Disputed lands

The Thirteen Colonies

NH
NY
MA
RI
CT
PA
NJ
DE
MD
VA
NC
SC
GA

ATLANTIC OCEAN

GULF OF MEXICO

PACIFIC OCEAN

George Washington was a young officer from Virginia. He went west to fight in the French and Indian War. He learned how to organize and lead soldiers. He would need these skills to help his country at a later time.

The French and Indian War

England and France were *rivals.* They both claimed the western land. Both countries sent soldiers to fight. They called the battles the French and Indian War because many Indian tribes joined the French. People in the English colonies feared the French and the Indians, so they helped the English soldiers.

Delaware's leaders created a *militia.* A militia is a group of men who join together to protect their property. The militia was formed to protect the colony if the French attacked.

The leaders voted to buy a new cannon for the fort at New Castle. They also sent money to help pay for an army to fight the French. The English were pleased. They thanked Delaware for its help in winning the war.

England Wins the War

After nine years of fighting, the war was over. England gained control of the land from the Atlantic Ocean to the Mississippi River. It also gained Canada. England now controlled most of North America.

The war had cost a lot of money. Parliament and the new English king, George III, looked for ways to pay the bills. They decided that because the American colonies got land in the west, the Americans should help pay for the war.

The Stamp Act

To raise money to pay for the war, the English Parliament *taxed* the colonists. A tax is money people have to pay to the government. The Stamp Act said the colonists had to buy stamps and put them on government and legal papers. Letters, newspapers, and even playing cards also had to have the stamps. The English made money on the sale of the stamps.

When news of the Stamp Act reached Delaware and the other colonies, the people were very angry. The colonists had helped the English in their war against the French. They had paid money to help win the war.

The colonists were not just angry about having to pay taxes. They were angry that they did not get to elect any members of Parliament. They had no one in England to represent their ideas. Only people in England voted for members of Parliament. That is why the colonists shouted, "No taxation without representation!"

The colonists held a meeting to talk about the Stamp Act. Delaware sent Caesar Rodney and Thomas McKean to the meeting. They both strongly *opposed* the Stamp Act. The men agreed to say "No" to Parliament and the king.

The English government had two parts—the king (or queen) and Parliament. Parliament was a group of men the people elected to make laws.

England's King George III and Parliament ruled the American colonies.

King George III

These are colonial playing cards. Cards were very popular, so they were taxed by the Stamp Act. The British hoped to make money from taxes on the playing cards.

The Delaware Adventure

Colonists were angry over the taxes. In this picture, they are arguing with the tax collectors.

New Laws from Parliament

Finally, England agreed to take back the Stamp Act. This did not mean England gave up its effort to raise tax money in America. Parliament passed a law to tax products that the colonists bought from England. They taxed glass, paper, paint, and tea.

John Dickinson wrote newspaper articles called "Farmer's Letters." The letters said Parliament had no right to tax the colonists. The letters made Dickinson famous throughout the colonies.

John Dickinson

John Dickinson was the son of Samuel Dickinson. You read about him in the last chapter. As a young man, John Dickinson went to London, England, to study law. When he returned to America he practiced law in Pennsylvania and in Delaware. He later helped write a new constitution for his country and his state.

LETTER FROM A FARMER, & LETTER I.

My dear COUNTRYMEN,

I AM a *Farmer*, settled, after a va of fortunes, near the banks of the Delaware, in the province of Pen vania. I received a liberal educat and have been engaged in the scenes of life; but am now convin nan may be as happy without bustle, as v tarm is small; my servants are few, and go little money at interest; I wish for no mor loyment in my own affairs is easy; and wit d grateful mind, undisturbed by wordly hop relating to myself, I am completing the nu vs allotted to me by divine goodness.

generally master of my time, I spend a goo in a library, which I think the most valua f my small estate; and being acquainted wit two or three gentlemen of abilities and learning, whe honour me with their friendship, I have acquired, believe, a greater knowledge in history, and the law and constitution of my country, than is generally at ained by men of my class, many of th fortunate

Creating a New Nation

Men dressed as Indians and climbed up on the English ship that carried tea. First they took the captain and crew below deck. Then they cracked open the heavy chests of tea leaves and dumped them overboard into the dark water below.

A Tea Party in Boston

People in Delaware and the other colonies refused to buy English goods. English merchants lost money when they couldn't sell English cloth, sugar, tea, and other things. Parliament finally agreed to give up all the taxes except for the tax on tea.

The English knew that Americans loved tea. They hoped the Americans would be willing to pay the tax in order to get it. The English sent ships full of tea to American ports. They tried to sell it at a low price. The Americans knew the cheap tea was a trick to get them to buy it and pay the tax.

In Boston, Massachusetts, a group of colonists dressed as Indians and boarded a ship that carried tea. They threw the tea overboard into the water below. This event was called the "Boston Tea Party."

The English were very angry. They closed the port of Boston. English soldiers were sent to control the Massachusetts Colony. This made the people of the colonies even more angry. Soon shops were empty of the things that used to come on ships. People could not buy and sell like they used to.

The Delaware Adventure

Colonists sent men to Philadelphia to make plans. How would they get rid of English rule?

Where Is Philadelphia?

Pennsylvania

Philadelphia ● NJ

Maryland

DE

Virginia

The Colonies Resist

People in all the colonies believed they must join together to resist the English government. They agreed to hold a meeting called a Continental Congress in Philadelphia. At the meeting they would decide how to unite against England.

Delaware sent three men to the meeting. They were Caesar Rodney, George Read, and Thomas McKean.

At the same time, England was sending more ships and soldiers across the ocean. They wanted to be ready if fighting broke out.

① MEMORY MASTER

1. What was the cause of the French and Indian War?
2. What country won the war?
3. What was the Stamp Act?
4. Why did the American colonies refuse to pay for the stamps?
5. How did the Boston Tea Party affect the colonists?

PEOPLE TO KNOW

Thomas Jefferson
Thomas McKean
George Read
Ceasar Rodney

PLACES TO LOCATE

Concord, Massachusetts
Lexington, Massachusetts
Philadelphia, Pennsylvania
Dover
New Castle

WORDS TO UNDERSTAND

constitution
illegal
revolution

*A **revolution** is when people try to overthrow their government and replace it with a new government.*

The War Begins

While the men of the Continental Congress were meeting in Philadelphia, the American Revolution started in Massachusetts. The first battles were at the towns of Lexington and Concord. Men on both sides fired. Men on both sides were killed and wounded.

News of the battles reached Philadelphia. The men at the Continental Congress agreed to raise an army to protect Americans from the English army. They appointed George Washington to be the army's commander.

Separation Day in Delaware

During the American Revolution, the men in Philadelphia asked the colonies to establish their own state governments. Delaware's leaders met in New Castle and voted to separate from England. They decided that they would not obey any English laws. They would not pay taxes to England.

Separation Day is now celebrated in New Castle every year on June 15. That was the day Delaware's leaders voted to separate from England.

Linking the Past to the Present

Every year, the people of our country celebrate the Fourth of July with parades, picnics, programs, and fireworks. The Fourth of July is our country's Independence Day. It is the day the leaders in the colony decided to break away from England with an official document called the Declaration of Independence.

Declaring Independence

The most important event of the American Revolution took place in July, 1776. A few weeks after Delaware's Separation Day, the leaders of all the colonies voted to break from England. They wanted to create a new nation called the United States of America.

Thomas Jefferson, from Virginia, wrote the Declaration of Independence. He explained that because the colonists had been treated unfairly, they were cutting all ties with England. He began with these famous words:

> *We hold these truths to be self-evident, that all men are created equal and that they are endowed by their Creator with certain unalienable rights, that among these are Life, Liberty, and the pursuit of Happiness.*

- A truth that is **self-evident** is one that any thoughtful person will understand and agree with.
- An **unalienable** right is one that no government can take away from you.

On July 4th, 1776, the document was ready. Later, men from all the colonies signed it. They sent it to England. Today, life in the United States is still based on these ideas.

Leaders from the colonies agreed to send a document to England. They declared they would no longer obey English laws.

Thomas Jefferson wrote the Declaration of Independence on this desk.

Caesar Rodney's *Ride*

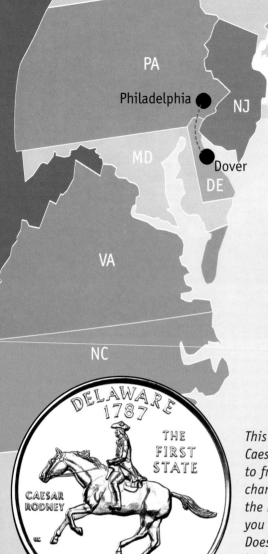

It was very important to get all the colonies to agree to separate from England. When it was time to vote, the men from Delaware were split. Thomas McKean was for independence. George Read was not sure the time was right. Caesar Rodney was for independence, but he was away on army business.

Once he heard that his vote was needed in Philadelphia, Caesar Rodney rode as fast as he could. He rode from his farm near Dover to cast his vote in Philadelphia. His ride is one of the most famous events in Delaware history. He had to ride all night through thunder and lightning storms. He rode along muddy roads and crossed flooded streams. He got to Philadelphia on July 2. He arrived just in time to vote for independence.

This modern quarter shows Caesar Rodney's famous ride to freedom. When you get change at the store, look at the new quarters and see if you can find one like this. Does the man on the horse look like the painting below?

Thomas McKean's *parents died when he was eight years old. He grew up and studied the law. McKean lived in New Castle and was a leader in Delaware. He also lived part of the time in Philadelphia and became an important judge there.*

George Read *became a lawyer in New Castle. At first, he held back from the idea of American independence. But when Thomas McKean and Caesar Rodney cast their votes for independence, he did the same.*

Delaware's First Constitution

Delaware and the other colonies joined together to form
a new nation called the United States of America. Then
Delaware needed a new state government. The state's
voters elected men to write a new **constitution.** It set up
rules for the voters to elect men to a General Assembly.

The Assembly was the most powerful part of the new
government. The men elected to the Assembly made the
laws. They also chose the judges for the state's courts. They
chose a president of the state. The president had few duties
except to be commander of the state militia. Today, our
state does not have a president. Instead, we have a governor.

First Steps Toward Ending Slavery

Many people thought that a state that was fighting a war
for freedom should not allow slavery. Delaware's new
constitution made it ***illegal*** to bring more slaves into the
state. The Constitution of 1776 said:

> *No person [brought] into this state from Africa ought to be
> held in slavery. And no slave ought to be brought into this
> state for sale from any part of the world.*

The constitution failed, however, to stop all slavery in the
state. It only stopped masters from buying more slaves from
other places. A few slave owners did free their slaves. A few
former slaves from Delaware served in the American army.
It would take many more years, however, before all the
slaves in Delaware were freed.

Tories and Patriots

People who wanted
freedom from England were
called Patriots. They
supported the Declaration
of Independence.

However, not all people
in Delaware wanted
independence. Some sided
with the English. They were
called Tories. The Tories
wanted Delaware to remain
a colony of England.

The Delaware State Seal

When the men in the General Assembly first met, one of their duties was to choose a new state seal. They wanted the seal to show what the American Revolution was about. They wanted the seal to show liberty fleeing from England to America. But their artist did not know how to draw a picture to show that idea.

The men then agreed to make a seal that would show what life in Delaware was like. They asked the artist to include a soldier and a farmer. They also asked for pictures of things that were often seen in the state. Those pictures are still on Delaware's state seal. Look at the seal. What do you see on it?

② MEMORY MASTER

1. What is Separation Day, and where is it celebrated?
2. Why did Caesar Rodney ride to Philadelphia?
3. Why do Americans celebrate the Fourth of July?

The English Attack

Even before the Declaration of Independence was signed, King George III sent a large army across the Atlantic Ocean to America. The English leader was Lord William Howe. The American army was led by George Washington.

The English soldiers fought colonists in Massachusetts and then attacked New York. The Americans fought hard to stop them, but the English won control of New York City. The English failed, however, to destroy Washington's army. Washington and his soldiers were going to fight on for their country's freedom.

The Delaware Continentals

Delaware sent between 700 and 800 **troops** (soldiers) to serve in the American army. They were called the Delaware Continentals. They were well-trained. They had good weapons and supplies. They fought bravely in every major campaign of the war.

When they set out from Delaware for New York, the soldiers looked very handsome in their blue coats with red trim, white vests, and buckskin pants called breeches. After many marches and battles, however, the fine clothing wore out.

By the end of the war only about 100 soldiers remained. They were dressed in rags, some "so naked as to be unfit for duty." Many of the soldiers had died. Others were too wounded or too sick to keep going.

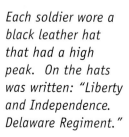

Each soldier wore a black leather hat that had a high peak. On the hats was written: "Liberty and Independence. Delaware Regiment."

The artist wanted his painting to show Washington leading his men out of a stormy darkness into a new dawn of freedom.

The Delaware Blue Hens

In their free time, American soldiers liked to see fights between roosters. These were called cockfights. Often roosters from different states fought each other.

The Delaware soldiers brought some very tough birds. They were called "the Blue Hens" because they had blue feathers. The blue hens usually won their fights.

Soldiers from other states said that Delaware's soldiers fought like their blue hens.

Fear of Invasion

Lord Howe's large, well-trained army drove Washington's army across New Jersey and into Pennsylvania. Then people in Delaware feared that the English army might *invade* their state.

Washington Crosses the Delaware River

Caesar Rodney's brother Thomas led a group of soldiers to come to Washington's aid. They grabbed their rifles and marched to join Washington in Pennsylvania.

On a freezing night, the men from Delaware took part in Washington's bold attack on the enemy. The Americans secretly crossed the Delaware River.

The river was very full of floating ice, and the wind was blowing very hard, and the night was very dark and cold, and we had great difficulty in crossing.

—*Thomas Rodney*

The Delaware Adventure

The next day they surprised the enemy in Trenton, New Jersey. The enemy troops were celebrating Christmas and were not expecting an attack. After a short battle, they surrendered. Washington took prisoners back across the river to Philadelphia. Then Washington moved on to attack at Princeton. The Americans won again.

The victories gave the Americans new hope that they could win the war. The victories also meant that the English would not attack Pennsylvania and Delaware, at least not yet.

The English Capture Philadelphia and Wilmington

Then Lord Howe decided to capture Philadelphia. He put his army, cannon, and horses into 230 ships. The huge fleet sailed from New York City down the coast and up the Chesapeake Bay. General Washington climbed Iron Hill near Newark to watch the enemy land.

The English marched into Delaware near Glasgow. A small group of soldiers attacked them at Cooch's Bridge. This was the only Revolutionary War battle fought in Delaware.

You can read the words on this marker if you visit Cooch's Bridge. Delaware's only battle of the American Revolution was fought here.

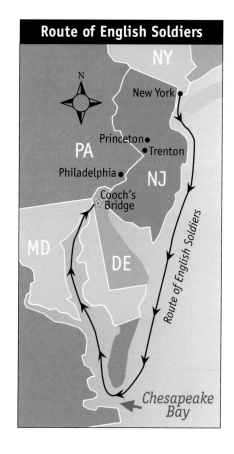

Route of English Soldiers

Creating a New Nation

The English captured this flag of the Delaware Continentals at the Battle of Brandywine.

Lord Howe's troops brushed off the Americans and kept moving on through Newark. Then Washington's whole army attacked as the English crossed the Brandywine River in Pennsylvania. But the English kept coming at them. Finally the English won the Battle of Brandywine. They captured Philadelphia and Wilmington.

Dr. John McKinly, the president of Delaware, lived in Wilmington. He tried to escape to a ship, but the English captured the ship. The ship also had a chest of money. The General Assembly had hidden the state's money on the ship. They thought it would be safer there. They were wrong!

The Government Moves to Dover

The English navy now controlled the Delaware Bay and the river. New Castle was no longer a safe place for the state government. The government offices were moved from New Castle to Dover. Delaware's government has stayed in Dover ever since.

The English Leave Wilmington

The English soldiers did not stay in Wilmington for long. They spent the winter in Philadelphia in warm houses while the American army froze in tents at Valley Forge.

George Read's Escape

George Read was in Philadelphia when the English army captured the city. He escaped by boat across the Delaware River into New Jersey, where his family was staying. Soon the Reads wanted to return to their home in New Castle. They got a boat to take them across the river.

Unfortunately, an English patrol boat came along and demanded to know who they were. If the English had found out that George Read was a government leader, he would have been arrested. However, he fooled the English sailors so well that the sailors helped the family unload their baggage on the shore. Then the Reads went home.

The Delaware Adventure

Women and Children Helped

Some of the hardest work women did was to stay at home and work on the farm while the men were off in battle. Without the women who planted and harvested the crops, Americans would have starved. The children also had to work hard. They had to feed animals and milk cows. They worked long hours in the fields with their mothers. They took care of younger children so their mothers would have more time to farm.

Some women went with their husbands to the army camps. They cooked, washed, and mended the soldier's clothes. They took care of wounded soldiers. They wrote letters for soldiers who wanted to send messages to their own wives and children at home.

Women took care of the farms while the men were in the army.

Nancy Hanson Saves an American Officer

After the Battle of the Brandywine, English soldiers came to Wilmington and took over the town. An American army officer was also in town. He needed to escape. Nancy Hanson lived in Wilmington and hid the frightened soldier in her house. She hid his uniform under the red bricks in front of her fireplace. Then she invited an English army officer to breakfast. While they were eating, Nancy bravely said she needed to go across the street to get some clothes for a sick relative.

Nancy quickly ran across the street and got a man's nightshirt from her neighbor. She took it home and secretly gave it to the American officer to wear. Then she asked the English officer if her sick relative could leave town. He agreed. Nancy put the American soldier, dressed in the nightshirt, into a carriage. The carriage carried him across the river to safety. The English officer never knew he had been fooled!

Benjamin Franklin

Benjamin Franklin began his career as a printer in Philadelphia. He wrote and printed *Poor Richard's Almanac*. It had many wise and funny sayings. He also printed the first book of Delaware's laws. Later, he was the oldest man to sign the U.S. Constitution.

Franklin was also an inventor and scientist. In his most famous experiment he flew a kite during a lightening storm. He tied a key on the kite string. When lightening struck the key, Franklin proved that lightening was really electricity. He thought the electricity could be controlled to work for people. He used this knowledge to invent the lightening rod. It carried electricity down into the ground so it would not burn a building if it struck the roof.

Franklin invented many other things, too. Try to learn about some of them.

France Helps the Colonists

The Americans knew that France and England were enemies. Benjamin Franklin went to France and asked for help to **defeat** the English. Americans needed more weapons, more ships, and more soldiers.

Benjamin Franklin was well-known and respected in France. He got the French to agree to send over 5,000 soldiers and a great fleet of ships to help the Americans.

Battle of Yorktown

General Washington led the American and French armies to Yorktown, Virginia. French ships blocked the Chesapeake Bay. They cut off any chance of the English troops getting help. The English were trapped by land and by sea! The English general sent a man to surrender to George Washington. The American Revolution was finally over.

Surrender at Yorktown

PA
NJ
MD
DE
VA
Yorktown •
N

③ MEMORY MASTER

1. Who were the Delaware Continentals?
2. Why were General Washington's surprise attacks at Trenton and Princeton important?
3. How did France help the Americans win the war?

The New United States

The United States of America was now a free country. The soldiers who had survived the war came home. The people could now work for the blessings of liberty for which so many had fought and died.

Washington Leads the New Country

George Washington had done a wonderful job leading the army. Some people wanted to make him a king, but Washington believed the people should vote for a president.

Washington told the people he wanted to go home to Virginia. After so many years away from home, he just wanted to be with his wife, Martha, and run their large plantation.

Problems with the National Government

Government leaders had a new country to run. But the United States government did not have enough power to rule a nation. The government did not have the power to tax the people. There was no money to run the country. There was not even enough money to pay the soldiers who had fought in the war.

There were other problems. Each state could tax products being bought or sold to other states. People in Delaware bought things from larger states such as Pennsylvania. What would happen if Pennsylvania put a large tax on those goods? That would make things cost more.

Another problem was that each state had its own kind of money. Can you think of what it would be like to have different bills and coins in every state?

Something had to be done. The U.S. government needed more power to help the states work together.

PEOPLE TO KNOW

Richard Bassett
Gunning Bedford
Jacob Broom
John Dickinson
George Read
George Washington

WORDS TO UNDERSTAND

compromise
delegate
federal
legislature
population
ratify

Once again, George Washington was asked to help his country. He rode a horse into Philadelphia to lead the convention. Find George Washington. Find Benjamin Franklin sitting in the front. Men from Delaware are also in the painting, but it is hard to know who they are. You can see their pictures below.

No picture exists of Jacob Broom, another delegate from Delaware.

The Constitutional Convention

About six years after the war ended, the states again sent *delegates* to Philadelphia. The delegates had been elected by the people to speak for their whole state. The men wanted a stronger United States government. They had a meeting that lasted many days. They decided that the new nation needed an entirely new set of rules. They started to talk about a new Constitution.

Delaware sent five delegates. The two most famous were George Read and John Dickinson. Delaware's other delegates were Jacob Broom, a manufacturer, Richard Bassett, a wealthy farmer, and Gunning Bedford, Jr., a lawyer.

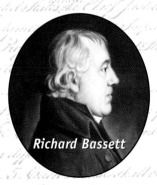

Richard Bassett

Gunning Bedford

George Read

John Dickinson

The Great Compromise

The new Constitution had to solve many problems. There were many disagreements between the states that had a lot of people and the states that had fewer people. The states with a high *population* were thought of as the large states, no matter how much land they had. The states with a lower population were thought of as the small states, no matter how much land they had.

Delaware was a small state. The delegates wanted a stronger United States government, but they did not want to let the large states have all the power. They did not want the large states to have more votes when laws were made.

After much argument over many days, the large and small states agreed to a *compromise.* A compromise is an agreement where each side gives in a little so an agreement can be made.

The compromise created a *legislature,* or Congress, that would make the laws. The legislature would have two parts. They would be called the Senate and the House of Representatives. Here is how it would work:

- **The Senate:** Every state would send two members. Delaware would have as many senators as large states such as Pennsylvania and New York.

- **The House of Representatives:** Every state would send representatives based on the population of the state. Large states would have more members than small states.

The Constitution was written with a feather pen like this one. The pen was dipped into ink over and over again.

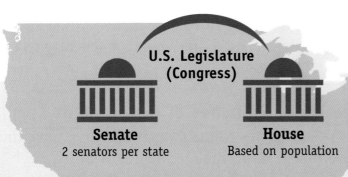

U.S. Legislature (Congress)

Senate
2 senators per state

House
Based on population

Delaware's leaders ratified the new Constitution at an inn in Dover.

The First State

A certain number of states had to **ratify,** or approve, the new Constitution before it could go into effect. Leaders in Delaware were so eager to ratify that they beat the other states. Delaware became the first state to ratify the new Constitution. That is why our license plate says "The First State."

Delaware Day

In early December, Delaware's voters elected delegates to meet at another convention. This one met in Dover. Because there was no building where they could meet, the delegates met in an inn. The delegates agreed to ratify the United States Constitution "fully, freely, and completely." We still celebrate Delaware Day on December 7th every year.

Federal and State Governments

The new United States government was called the *federal* government. It was a government of all the states. The Constitution gave the federal government power over some things such as making war and peace, printing money, and collecting taxes.

The Constitution also said the states would keep the power to do many things for themselves. This was important to the states. They didn't want the federal government to have all the power.

The Three Branches of Government

The delegates to the Constitutional Convention created a government with three branches, or parts. Each branch has its own jobs, or power. This is called "separation of power."

Each branch is a check upon the powers of the other two. This means no person or part of the government can seize all the power. This is called "checks and balances."

- The legislature, called Congress, is one branch.
- The president is head of another branch.
- The courts make up a third branch.

You will learn more about the branches of government in a later chapter.

The New Government Begins

After about a year, enough states had ratified the Constitution. The new government could begin. George Washington was everyone's choice to be the first president of the United States. Delaware and the other states elected men to the new Congress. President Washington chose judges to serve in the courts. The new government was underway.

The Bill of Rights

One of the first things the new Congress did was to propose a series of amendments, or additions, to the Constitution to protect the rights of American citizens. The first 10 amendments are called the Bill of Rights. They include the right to freedom of religion, speech, and the press. The leaders wanted to make sure that no government could ever take these rights away from Americans. You will read more about the Bill of Rights in a later chapter.

④ MEMORY MASTER

1. What did the men at the Constitutional Convention do?
2. How did Delaware become the First State?

President Washington Visits Delaware

The new government offices were located first in Philadelphia and then in New York City. George Washington passed through Delaware many times as he traveled from his home in Virginia to Philadelphia and New York.

A little girl in Wilmington named Betsy Montgomery wrote that she once climbed a tree to see the president pass by.

It was a day of great expectation when his chariot appeared, driving slowly through the crowd, he bowing, hat in hand, and with handkerchiefs waving, and every face flushed, and eyes sparkling with joy. Then a shout, "Did you see General Washington? Yes! He bowed to me!"

CHAPTER 4 REVIEW

From There to Here

The colonies refused to pay the English taxes. Leaders from the colonies joined together to decide what to do. Thomas Jefferson wrote the Declaration of Independence. It told England that the colonies would no longer belong to England. This was the first step toward creating the United States of America.

Most people in Delaware supported the call for independence, and Delaware people served bravely through the American Revolution. Some of the Delaware Continentals were with George Washington when he crossed the icy Delaware River on Christmas Eve. Women at home did whatever they could to help win a war.

About six years after the long war was over, leaders again met in Philadelphia. They wrote the United States Constitution to make a stronger government. Delaware was the first state to ratify the new Constitution.

What Do You Remember?

1. Why did the American colonies refuse to pay English taxes?
2. What are the opening words of the Declaration of Independence?
3. Why was Caesar Rodney important?
4. What country helped the colonies win the American Revolution?
5. Why is Delaware called "The First State"?
6. Who was the first president of the United States of America?

Geography Tie-In

On a world map, find all of the countries in this chapter. How did people travel from one place to another? Find out how long it took soldiers and others to travel across the Atlantic Ocean on sailing ships.

The Delaware Adventure

Technology Tie-In

Two major technologies of the American Revolution were the printing press and the rifle. Do some research to learn more about these things. Use your library or the Internet. Why were they important to the people at the time? How have they changed? Are they still important today?

Activity

Draw a Picture of Washington's Visit

Draw a picture based on Betsy Montgomery's words about President George Washington's visit to Wilmington. Write a title for the picture. Try to draw the children in the picture dressed in clothes of the time period. Try to draw President Washington dressed like the paintings of him in this chapter or in other books you can find in the library.

"*Manufacturers are bees in peace, hornets in war.*"

—Du Pont Company
Workers' Banner, 1813

Timeline of Events

1790
Oliver Evans uses his new
machinery in flour mills.

1792
Delaware adopts a
new constitution.

1813
The English navy
attacks Lewes.

1790   **1800**   **1810**

1802
The Du Pont Powder Mills open.

1812-1815
War of 1812

1803
The Louisiana Purchase adds
land to the United States.

Life and Work in the New State

The Brandywine River provided swiftly moving water to run machines in the mills. Later, steam power replaced water power in the mills.

1817
The Newport-Gap Turnpike is completed.

1832
The New Castle and Frenchtown Railroad begins to operate.

1840
A peach boom begins.

1856
The Delaware Railroad reaches Seaford.

1820   1830   1840   1850   1860

1829
• Public schools begin.
• The Chesapeake and Delaware Canal opens.

1838
The Philadelphia, Wilmington, and Baltimore Railroad begins to operate.

1846-1849
The Mexican War adds land to the United States.

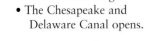

103

LESSON ①

A New Constitution for Delaware

PEOPLE TO KNOW

Samuel Davis
Thomas Jefferson
Jacob Jones

PLACES TO LOCATE

England
France
Dover
Lewes
Delaware Bay

WORDS TO UNDERSTAND

bombardment
confidence
refuse

Some leaders in Delaware thought the state's first constitution had been written too quickly. They wanted to make it better. Each of Delaware's three counties sent 10 delegates to Dover. The 30 men worked together to write the new constitution. The new constitution made these important changes:

- The state's name was changed from "the Delaware State" to "the State of Delaware." That is still the name of our state today.
- The title of the state's top leader was changed from "president" to "governor." He would be elected by the people. The new constitution gave the governor more power.
- The names of the two houses of the General Assembly would be the "Senate" and the "House of Representatives."

The first copy of the 1792 state constitution looked like this.

The Constitution of the State of Delaware.

We, the People, hereby ordain and establish this Constitution of Government for the State...

104   *The Delaware Adventure*

Who Could Vote?

The new constitution said that only white men who paid taxes could vote. White men no longer had to own property to be able to vote. That made it easier for poor white men to vote.

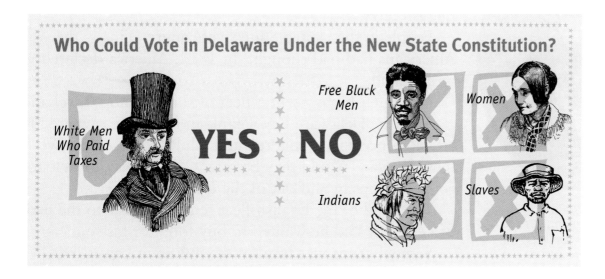

Who Could Run the Government?

The new constitution said that white men of any religion could be in government. Before that, only Protestants could help run the government. Catholics, Jews, and people of other religious groups could now hold government offices.

What do you think?

- Why do you think certain groups of people were not allowed to vote?
- Compare Delaware's voting rules to our voting rules today.
- Should a person's religion keep him or her from holding a government office?

Another War with England

Across the ocean in Europe, England and France were fighting each other. Then both sides attacked American ships in the ocean. England was very daring. The English stopped American ships and made the American sailors join the English navy.

People in the United States were angry. Finally the Americans had had enough. In 1812, America declared war on England.

The English navy sent a fleet of ships to stop travel and trade in the Delaware Bay. People in Delaware prepared for attack. Once again, children and adults were scared. Would there be war? Would they be safe? Would they be able to get their ships in and out of the Delaware Bay?

The head of the English fleet sent a message to the people of Lewes. It said he wanted to buy food for his soldiers.

Samuel Davis was head of the militia in Lewes. He *refused* to sell food to the enemy. Then the English said their navy would attack the town if they could not buy food.

General Samuel Boyer Davis ordered his men in Lewes to fire English cannonballs right back at them!

The Attack on Lewes

The English fired 241 cannons at the town. This *bombardment* by cannonballs and burning rockets went on for 22 hours. The English goal was to knock down or burn down all of the houses and stores in Lewes.

Lewes had only four cannons and a few cannonballs, but the people were very lucky. They soon saw that the English ships were too far away for the cannonballs to hit the homes and stores. Instead, the cannonballs were landing on the beach in front of the town.

The boys of the town ran down to the beach to collect the cannonballs and brought them back into town. Then General Davis ordered his men to fire the used cannonballs back at the English ships!

The English fire rockets did not hurt Lewes, either. They sailed over the town and landed in fields.

These cannons defended Lewes.

The Delaware Adventure

Damage to Lewes

The bombardment of Lewes was very loud and long. Again, the people of Lewes were lucky. No buildings had been knocked down. No people had been hurt. Only one cannonball hit a house, and it is still there today. The next time you are in Lewes, go and see the Cannonball House.

The people of Lewes were proud of how they had worked together to save their town. When the English saw that they could not destroy Lewes, they stopped shooting and sailed out of Delaware Bay.

One Delaware soldier wrote a funny sentence that said:

The commodore and all his men,
shot a dog and killed a hen.

A commodore was a leader in the navy. What do you think the man who wrote the funny saying was trying to say about the success of the attack on Lewes?

The Cannonball House still stands at the Lewes Marine Museum.

Lewes •

Jacob Jones, American Hero

Jacob Jones grew up in Lewes. He was a doctor, but he loved the sea more than medicine. He joined the navy.

Jacob Jones won one of the first American victories against the English navy in the War of 1812. He was captain of a ship called the *Wasp*. He led his men to capture a much larger English ship. The victory helped raise the **confidence** of the Americans in their fight against the English. Captain Jones's victory made him a hero.

The War Is Over

The War of 1812 went on for several years, but when it was over, the people of Delaware celebrated. They lit candles, fired guns, and cheered for peace. Since that time, Delaware has never been attacked by an enemy.

······· **Activity** ·······

From Sea to Shining Sea

Over the years, the United States got more and more land. President Thomas Jefferson hoped to expand the United States westward. Americans could move to this new land and create more states. President Jefferson bought the Louisiana Territory from France. This huge land region stretched from the Mississippi River to the Rocky Mountains.

1. Compare this map and a modern map of the United States. What states were once owned by France?
2. Later, after a war with Mexico, the United States got land in the West. What states were once part of Mexico?
3. Many pioneers went west to Oregon Country. What modern states were once part of that land region?

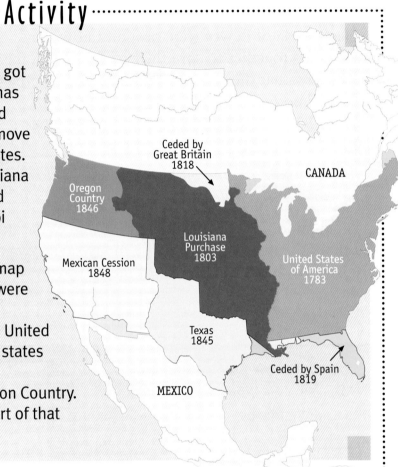

The Delaware Adventure

Population Growth

Delaware's population grew, but it did not grow as fast as other states. In fact, in some years, it did not grow at all. Many people left Delaware because they could not make a living. They moved west to new places as far away as California and Oregon.

Not everyone left to find work. Some people stayed and worked on their farms. A few people were doctors and lawyers. Some owned stores and mills. New people came to Wilmington to find jobs in mills and factories. Some came from other states. Some came from Ireland and Germany in hopes of finding good jobs.

Family Life

People spent a lot of time with their families. Whole families worked together. Some worked in factories. Others worked on farms.

People made many of the things they used. Most women made clothes for their family. Men helped each other build houses and barns.

Women and girls sewed scraps together to make quilts.

William Frazer was a wealthy farmer. He owned a lot of land and many animals. He was so proud of his farm that he had a view of it painted as part of his portrait.

Farming the Land

Farmers grew grains such as corn, wheat, and oats. They also had vegetable gardens and fruit trees. They raised animals. Farming was hard work. Farmers started working before sunrise and stopped working after the sun set. If a farmer could afford it, he would hire extra workers or use slaves to help.

On the farm, boys helped their fathers in the fields and with the animals. Mothers and daughters cooked, cleaned, and took care of the gardens. They canned fruit in jars for the winter. They dried meat so it would not spoil. They also made soap and candles. At harvest time even the mothers and daughters had to work in the fields.

Meet the Springer Family

Thomas Springer and his family lived on a farm near Hockessin. The family worked very hard. They had a good life, but they were not rich.

The Springer house was made of logs. It had two floors, with one room on each floor. Thomas and Elizabeth Springer lived in the house with their two daughters, Mary and Ann. Thomas owned four slaves. Their names were Ace, Will, Sara, and Amclia. The slaves lived in a separate building.

Everyone worked. The men worked in the fields and took care of the sheep, cows, and horses. The women took care of the chickens and the garden. They made butter from some of the cows' milk. They also cooked, cleaned, and sewed.

The family worked so hard that they did not have much free time. They might visit with family and friends or travel to New Castle or Wilmington. The towns were not far away, but travel was very slow. Still, going to town was an adventure!

Compare the Springer farm with the Frazer farm on the previous page.

> ### Linking the Past to the Present
>
> - How did the Springer family spend their free time?
> - How does your family spend its free time?

Hockessin
Wilmington
New Castle

Going to Church

Religion played a big part in the lives of most people. Churches tried to make life better for people. Men, women, and children learned to read in Sunday schools.

One of the largest church groups in the United States actually began in Delaware. Francis Asbury came from England to preach. The religion he taught was called Methodism. Many people who heard him teach became Methodists.

The Methodist Church soon became the largest religious group in Delaware. Both black people and white people went to Methodist churches.

Camp Meetings

Methodists held camp meetings. People came to a camp meeting and stayed for several days. They prayed together and listened to preaching. The preachers stood on a wooden platform so everyone could see and hear them. At night everyone slept in their wagons or tents. How do you think the children felt about going to camp meetings?

Francis Asbury

Barratt's Chapel is the place where the Methodist Church began in the United States. The church is still standing near Frederica.

The Delaware Adventure

Going to School

For many years only rich children went to school. There were no free public schools in Delaware. Then the state government passed a law that created public schools. Sadly, only white children could go to the new public schools.

Children had to walk to school. Each school had only one room and one teacher. The teacher taught geography, history, reading, writing, and arithmetic to children of all ages. Many schools did not have desks. Instead, children sat on long benches.

The school year was not very long. Farm children had too much work to do at home. Children who worked in mills and factories sometimes could not go to school at all.

Shopping at the General Store

A general store sold all kinds of things. A family could buy everything from needles and thread to cloth, nails, dishes, and shoes. People could also buy coffee, tea, chocolate, and other things from around the world.

Activity

Compare and Contrast Prices

Here are some goods and their prices from a general store:

Broom . . . . 13 1/2 cents	Bacon . . . . 11 cents per pound
Candles . . . . 2 1/2 cents	Rice . . . . 8 cents per pound
Cotton cloth . . . 12 1/2 cents per yard	Cheese . . . . 12 1/2 cents per pound
Writing paper . . 2 cents per sheet	Eggs . . . . 10 cents per dozen
Ink . . . . 15 cents per bottle	Tea . . . . 1 dollar per pound
Bonnet . . . . 87 1/2 cents	Bread . . . . 11 cents per loaf
Men's boots . . . 6 dollars 50 cents	Cantaloupe . . . . 6 cents each

Compare prices then and now. Are today's prices higher or lower? Are there any items you cannot find in a modern store? Why?

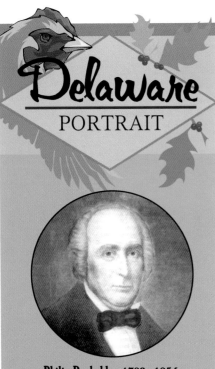

Delaware PORTRAIT

Philip Reybold • 1783–1854

As a young man, Philip Reybold moved near Delaware City. He first worked as a farmer. Then he worked as a brick maker. He sold his bricks in Philadelphia and New York City. He became very rich.

Then Reybold started growing peaches. He bought land for peach orchards all around Delaware City. Soon he had planted over 100,000 trees. He also asked other farmers to plant peach trees. Then he bought their peaches. He shipped all of those beautiful Delaware peaches by boat to the big cities of Philadelphia, Baltimore, and New York. People there couldn't get enough of the delicious fruit.

Philip Reybold became so successful that people called him the "Peach King."

The Peach Boom Begins

Peach trees had always grown well in Delaware. Many farmers had a few trees to provide fruit for their family. Then Isaac Reeves planted many peach trees in an *orchard* near Delaware City. An orchard is a field of fruit trees.

Mr. Reeves wanted to sell peaches to people who lived in the cities. They did not have enough land to plant their own trees. Soon a new business started in Delaware. Farmers who lived near the Delaware River shipped their golden yellow peaches by boat to Wilmington, Philadelphia, and even New York City. The peach business grew so fast it was called a "peach boom."

2 MEMORY MASTER

1. What was a general store?
2. What types of work did farm boys and girls do?
3. Describe an early public school.
4. How did religion affect the lives of the people?
5. Who bought Delaware's peaches? Why?

The Delaware Adventure

A Transportation Revolution

In the early years, travel was slow and hard. Then people found amazing new ways to travel. The new ways were so important and so different that we say the country went through a "transportation revolution."

Once people could travel faster and easier, life changed quickly. People could visit other places. They could see their families who lived in another city. Farmers could make money by shipping their grain, vegetables, and fruit to faraway places. They could buy things that other people made or grew.

Bad Roads

Do you remember reading in the last chapter about Caesar Rodney's ride from his farm in Delaware to Philadelphia? He made the long, hard trip to vote for independence. In Caesar Rodney's time there were only dirt roads. They were dusty in good weather. They were muddy when it rained.

The roads had deep holes in them. One writer told about a man whose horse stumbled. The horse threw the rider down into an eight-foot-deep hole. The man broke his leg, but the horse was not hurt.

It took a long time to travel from southern Delaware to northern Delaware on the bad roads.

This map from 1796 shows new roads built in Delaware.

PEOPLE TO KNOW

Davy Crockett

PLACES TO LOCATE

Clayton
Delaware City
Delmar
Dover
Harrington
Laurel
Middletown
New Castle
Newport
Seaford
Wilmington

WORDS TO UNDERSTAND

barge
canal
freight
lock
paddle wheel
toll
turnpike

115

This toll gate is on a turnpike near Wilmington. How does it compare to those on our modern turnpikes?

Turnpikes

To get better roads, companies built private roads called *turnpikes.* They charged a *toll,* or fee, to use them. Once a user paid the toll, a gatekeeper raised a wooden bar called a "pike." Turnpikes were better than regular roads because they had gravel and wooden planks covering places that might get muddy. The biggest users of turnpikes were farmers bringing their crops to the mills and markets in Wilmington.

The first turnpike in Delaware ran from Newport into Pennsylvania. Soon there were many turnpikes.

Traveling by Stagecoach

Stagecoaches could carry as many as 12 people. They had window openings, but the windows did not have glass in them. If it rained or snowed, the passengers had to pull down leather shades.

Stagecoaches ran between towns throughout Delaware. A traveler could go many places on the stagecoach, but it was not always easy. If the traveler boarded the stage in Milford, for example, he or she could go to Dover. Then the traveler could take a different stage to Wilmington. If the traveler wanted to go on to Philadelphia, it meant taking yet a third stagecoach.

Stagecoaches had trouble on the bad roads. Sometimes they turned over after hitting big holes. People and horses sometimes died in the accidents.

Traveling by Water

It was often easier to travel by water than on land. Small sailboats carried both goods and people on the Delaware River. The boats moved slowly.

Bigger sailboats could sail beyond the Delaware River into the ocean. Some sailing ships went as far as China.

This painting shows Lewes Harbor in 1784. How did the sails on these boats push them across the water? Can you see the lighthouse? It guided boats to the shore.

Aletta Clarke's Trip to Philadelphia, 1790

Aletta Clarke made a trip by sailboat from her home on Cedar Creek. It took her many days to get to Philadelphia. She was making the trip with two brothers and a cousin. Aletta kept a diary of what she did every day. This is what she wrote about her trip:

August 27 & 28: *We started for Philadelphia. The tide being very low, we could not go out.*

August 29: *Still could not get out.*

August 30: *The wind being in the East we came home.*

August 31: *We rode [by horse] down to the boat again.*

September 1: *About 1 o'clock we got out of the mouth of [Cedar] Creek. About 4 o'clock we struck [a sandbar], a very dangerous place. The wind blew fresh and the waters were in a great rage. Everybody on board was very much frightened, but [we got] through all danger.*

September 2: *Next morning we were [at] New Castle. About 4 o'clock we arrived a t Philadelphia.*

1. Where did Aletta start her trip? Where did she end her trip?
2. Why did she have so much trouble on the trip?
3. Can you think of a faster way she could have traveled?

Can you read what Aletta Clarke wrote on this page in her diary?

Steamboats on the Delaware River

The steamboat was a great invention. It did not have to rely on the wind to move. It used a steam engine. A steam engine is like a really big tea kettle. The steam from boiling water moves parts that turn a *paddle wheel*. The wheel turning in the water makes the boat move.

A steamboat could travel faster than a sailboat. It did not rely on the wind or have to go just the way a river flowed. A steamboat had enough power to go up or down a river on its own power.

People did not like the first steamboat launched on the Delaware River. Maybe the loud noises and the black smoke coming out of the smokestack scared them. Later on, people came to like steamboats. Steamboat companies offered service to towns along the Delaware River from Lewes to Wilmington. It was a great adventure to ride in a steamboat up and down the river.

The Steam-Boat

Superior,

CAPTAIN MILNER,

WILL commence running up and down daily, for the season, on Friday the 18th inst.

Leaving Wilmington at seven o'clock in the morning, And Philadelphia at two o'clock in the afternoon, (Sundays excepted.)

Passage one Dollar and twenty-five Cents. Freight at the same rate as charged by the Packets.

Wilmington, April 14, 1823.

For the accommodation of Friends going to yearly Meeting, the Boat will leave Wilmington, on Sunday morning, the 20th inst. and return in the afternoon.

Printed at the Gazette Office, 15, Market-street, Wilmington.

Where does this ad say the steamboat leaves from in the morning? Where does it leave from in the afternoon? How much did it cost to ride on the boat?

What kinds of boats do you see in this old drawing of the Wilmington waterfront?

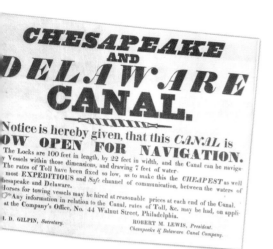

This poster advertised the Chesapeake and Delaware Canal.

The Chesapeake and Delaware Canal

For many years, businessmen wanted to make travel between the Chesapeake Bay and the Delaware River faster and cheaper. They wanted to build a *canal*. Canals are waterways dug by people. Boats on canals could carry people or heavy goods such as coal and iron.

It took a long time before a company could afford to build a canal across Delaware. The land rises in the middle of the state. How could the water flow uphill? It was too hard to shovel out the highest land down to sea level.

Instead, workers put in *locks.* A lock has gates at each end that can be used to raise or lower a boat. Then the boat can move up or down from one water level to another.

Canal Locks

Canals had "locks" to raise or lower boats along their journey. Follow the diagram to see how a canal lock worked.

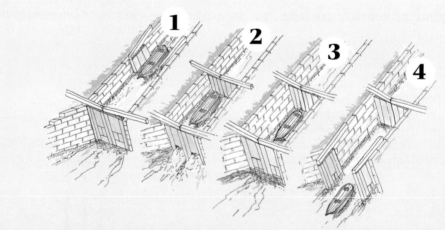

1. High water: a boat enters the lock.
2. The back gates close. Water is slowly let out of front gates.
3. The water level gets lower and lower.
4. The front gates open, and boat leaves the lock on a lower level.

Men Who Built the Canal

It took five years to build the 14-mile-long Chesapeake and Delaware Canal. The dirt had to be dug by hand with shovels. Then the dirt was loaded onto wagons. Horses hauled away the wagons full of dirt. Most of the men who dug out the canal were from Ireland. Some African Americans also helped dig the canal.

The workers lived in small wooden shacks. They worked long hours, even in bad weather.

Boats on the Canal

Two types of boats used the Chesapeake and Delaware Canal. Some were steamboats. Others had flat bottoms and were called *barges*. They carried heavy loads. Horses or mules walked along paths beside the canal and pulled the barges. Five or six horses or mules could pull a barge from one end of the canal to the other in just over two hours.

Linking the Past to the Present

After many years, the U.S. government took control of the canal. They made the canal wider. Then big ocean-going ships could pass through.

Chesapeake & Delaware Canal

Take a ride down the C&D Canal on this three-deck steamboat.

PENN

The Coming of the Railroads

The railroad was the most important and most exciting new type of transportation in the whole 19th century. Railroads began to connect all parts of the United States. The trains carried both people and *freight*. Freight is the many kinds of goods that are moved from place to place.

The New Castle and Frenchtown Railroad

The New Castle and Frenchtown Railroad was the first railroad to be built in Delaware. It was also one of the first to be built in America. It was not very long. It ran only 14 miles from New Castle, Delaware, to Frenchtown, Maryland. It connected the Delaware River to the Chesapeake Bay.

Although not long in miles, this little railroad cut many hours off the trip from Philadelphia to Baltimore. Before the railroad was built, travelers had to sail all the way down the Delaware River and then up the Chesapeake Bay.

The railroad began to carry passengers even before it got a steam engine to pull the train cars. The engine had to be sent in pieces from England and then put together in New Castle. Until the engine was ready, horses pulled the train cars along the tracks.

Train cars that looked like stage coaches were pulled along the tracks.

Davy Crockett, a Famous Passenger

Davy Crockett was from Tennessee. He was famous for his stories about the frontier. He was one of the early passengers on the New Castle and Frenchtown Railroad. Later, he wrote about his trip.

This was a clean new sight to me; about a dozen big stages hung on to one machine. . . . After a good deal of fuss, we all got seated and moved slowly off, the engine wheezing as if she had [a disease]. By-and-by she began to take short breaths, and away we went with a blue streak after us.

The Philadelphia, Wilmington, and Baltimore

The second railroad through Delaware was even more important because it carried both people and freight. This was the Philadelphia, Wilmington, and Baltimore Railroad. People used it to travel between those three cities and to other places. The railroad helped cities grow.

The Delaware Railroad

The farmers of Kent and Sussex Counties felt left out. They needed a railroad to help them get their crops to market. The Delaware Railroad was finally built.

The Delaware Railroad ran the full length of the state. It connected Wilmington with towns such as Middletown, Dover, Clayton, Harrington, Laurel, and Seaford. A big crowd waited for the first train to pull into the station in Seaford. Everyone cheered, and the town celebrated with a big feast.

Railroads made it easier for people to travel from city to city. Trains also carried goods to be sold in stores.

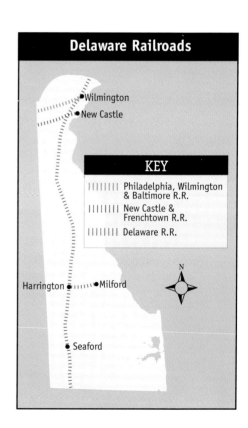

Delaware Railroads

- Wilmington
- New Castle

KEY

- ||||||| Philadelphia, Wilmington & Baltimore R.R.
- ||||||| New Castle & Frenchtown R.R.
- ||||||| Delaware R.R.

- Harrington
- Milford
- Seaford

N

3 MEMORY MASTER

1. Why was a turnpike better than other roads?
2. Why was a steamboat better than a sailboat?
3. What is a canal?
4. How did railroads help people?

Life and Work in the New State

E. I. du Pont
Oliver Evans
Joshua Gilpin
Thomas Gilpin

Newport
Rocky Mountains
Brandywine River
Mississippi River

inventor
manufacturing

Building Mills and Factories

Before the American Revolution, the colonists bought most of their goods from England. Then, after the United States became a new country, the people wanted to make their own goods. Making things people need is called *manufacturing*.

New mills and factories used many kinds of machines. The machines helped make things more quickly and cheaply than they could be made by hand. The time when many machines in factories and mills made goods came to be known as the "Industrial Revolution."

Some of the most important early mills and factories were in Delaware. They made such things as cloth, paper, tools, railroad cars, and gunpowder.

Machines Replace Men in the Flour Mills

You have already learned about the early mills that ground grain into flour. It took many men to turn grain into flour. They were called millers. Much of the work was very hard. Men had to carry heavy sacks of grain to the top of the mill. Then they dumped the grain into a bin that fed the grinding stones.

Workers manufactured all kinds of products in these mills on the Brandywine River.

Then Oliver Evans invented a system of machines that could do the work of most of the men in a large flour mill. He put buckets, or pockets, on a leather belt. The moving belt carried the grain from the ground to the top of the mill. Other machines moved the grain and flour through the mill.

The new machines made milling faster and cheaper. Five men using the new machines could produce as much flour as it had taken 20 men without the machines.

The Brandywine Flour Mills

At first the owners of the big flour mills along the Brandywine River would not buy the new machines. They called the machines "rattletraps" because they made a lot of loud noise. But when the millers did buy the machines, they were very happy with them. The machines rattled and banged day and night, all week long, but the Brandywine millers made the best flour in America. Many people came to visit the famous mills.

Machines made work at the flour mills much easier. Workers could make more flour in less time.

Delaware
PORTRAIT

Oliver Evans · 1755–1819

Oliver Evans was born in Newport. He loved machines, and soon he became an *inventor.* An inventor is someone who finds new ways to do things. Oliver Evans built machines and tools that made work easier for people.

Evans was Delaware's first great inventor. Day and night, he thought about how to make machines for a flour mill. Sometimes it seemed to be an impossible job, but he could not stop thinking about it.

In addition to his machines for flour mills, Oliver Evans built one of the first steam engines in America. He put the engine into a flat-bottomed boat. He added wheels and a paddlewheel and then drove the machine on the road and in the water. Sadly, no one bought his steam engine.

President Jefferson, on the right, talks to E.I. du Pont, on the left. The other men are on the president's staff.

Du Pont's Black Powder Mills

E.I. du Pont had learned how to make black powder in France. It was used to blast open coal mines. It was used to blast away rock when building canals, railroads, and roads. It was also used in war as ammunition. When du Pont saw how bad American powder was, he decided to build powder mills in America. He chose to build his mills on the Brandywine River near Wilmington. The river could provide the waterpower needed to run the mills.

The Du Pont Powder Mills became the most famous mills in Delaware. President Thomas Jefferson said the black powder was the best in the country. So did most other people. During the War of 1812 the Du Pont mills sold powder to the American army and navy.

Making Black Powder

Making powder was dangerous work. Du Pont built his mills outside of town so that if the powder blew up it would not kill the people in the town. The workers at the powder mills had to be very careful not to light a fire or even to make a spark.

The men had to wear shoes put together with wooden pegs instead of nails. Metal nails hitting a stone might make a spark that would start a huge explosion.

Powder mills had a special design. Each mill had three thick stone walls. The fourth wall was made only of wood, and it faced the river. A roof slanted down toward the water. If there were an explosion in the mill, the blast would blow out the wooden wall and send the powder, the machines, and sometimes even the mill workers across the river. You can see these mill buildings today if you visit the Hagley Museum.

The Gilpin brothers built their mills on the Brandywine River.

Gilpin Paper Mills

Two brothers, Thomas and Joshua Gilpin, also built mills on the Brandywine River. Their mills made paper. At first, paper had to be made one sheet at a time. To speed things up, the Gilpin brothers used a new machine that made paper in long rolls. Machines made paper faster and cheaper than the old way.

Steam power ran boats, machines in factories, and even the train in this picture. How many places in this picture of Wilmington show steam power at work? What products might be made in the factories?

From Waterpower to Steam

For years, waterwheels provided energy to run machines in factories. Then factory owners started using steam engines in their mills or factories. Most of the steam-powered mills and factories were in Wilmington. Many of these steam-powered factories made big things such as railroad cars or steamboats.

Working in the Mills

Men, women, and children worked in many of the mills and factories in Delaware. The work was hard and the hours were long. The people usually only got Sundays off. The rest of the time, they worked for 12 or more hours every day.

Mills and factories were noisy and dirty. Workers had to be careful and pay attention. If they were not, they lost fingers, arms, or legs in the machines. They might even be killed.

In a later chapter, you will read how people worked to make life better for workers.

4 MEMORY MASTER

1. Why did millers call the machines in a flour mill "rattletraps"?
2. What did Oliver Evans do?
3. What did E.I. du Pont make?
4. How did the Gilpin brothers change papermaking?

From There to Here

Even after their victory in the American Revolution, Americans had to fight England one more time. Delaware men had to fight in the War of 1812. They also had to make some changes in the state constitution.

Delaware was part of two other "revolutions." They were the transportation revolution and the industrial revolution. Inventors and their machines helped make travel and manufacturing easier and faster.

Life was not easy for most people in Delaware. Some left the state to seek their fortunes in the West. New people came to Delaware from Ireland and other countries. Their hard work helped build the state.

What Do You Remember?

1. What country did the United States fight against in the War of 1812?
2. Who won the bombardment of Lewes?
3. What was the peach boom?
4. How did canals help transportation?
5. Why were railroads important to the people of Delaware?
6. Name three products that were made in factories.

Activity

Inventions Make Life Easier

During the Industrial Revolution, many inventions improved people's lives. Machines did hard jobs much faster than people could do them.

Use different sources to learn more about the invention of the steam engine, the steamboat, or trains. Then write a short report or make a poster that shows what you found. You will want to learn about the inventor, how his invention worked, and where it was first used.

Population Graph

Population figures for Delaware are shown on a bar graph. You can use a bar graph to compare information.

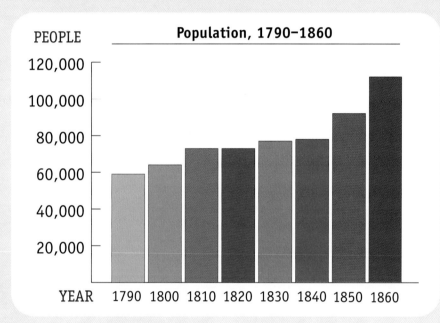

Population, 1790–1860

1. Did the number of people rise or fall from 1790 to 1860?

2. Review page 109 to see why the state's population stayed about the same for many years.

3. In what decade (10-year period) did the number of people living in Delaware increase the most?

Geography 🌐 Tie-In

On an outline map of the state, mark the following towns:

- Lewes, Georgetown, Seaford, Delmar, Dover, Middletown, Delaware City, New Castle, Newport, and Wilmington
- Philadelphia, Pennsylvania; and Baltimore, Maryland
- Where you live

Then talk with your class about how you would travel from your town to Philadelphia or Baltimore in 1850. Look at the canal and railroad maps in this chapter. Would you take a train? A turnpike? A canal boat? Would you have to ride a horse, or walk? What route would you take?

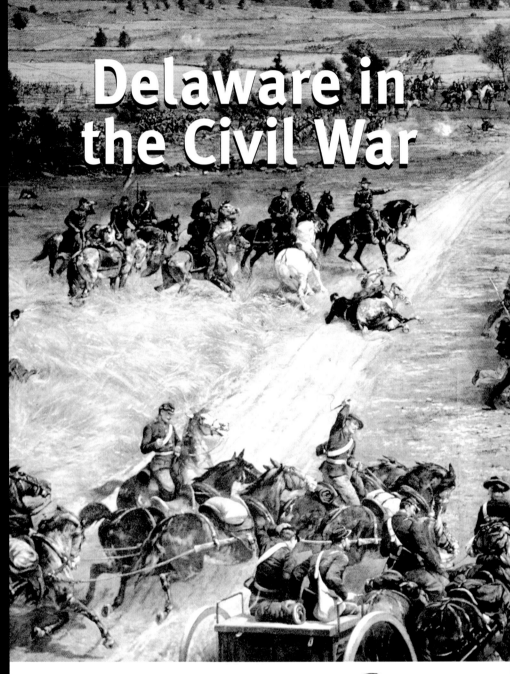

Delaware in the Civil War

" We are in the midst of a revolution that must decide the future of our country, and is most important to the destinies of humanity— the excitement and interest is intense."

—Anna Ferris, 1861

Timeline of Events

1830

1831
A slave revolt in Virginia leads to harsh laws against black people.

1835

1840

AM I NOT A MAN AND A BROTHER?

One of the most famous battles of the Civil War happened at Gettysburg, Pennsylvania. For three days soldiers fought there. What does this painting tell you about how wars were fought back then?

1848
Thomas Garrett is found guilty of helping slaves escape.

1863
• The Emancipation Proclamation frees slaves in the Confederacy.
• Battle of Gettysburg

1867
Schools for African American children are built throughout Delaware.

1845 1850 1855 1860 1865

1849
Harriet Tubman escapes and travels through Delaware.

1850
Fugitive Slave Law

1860
• Abraham Lincoln is elected president of the United States.
• The Southern States form the Confederate States of America.

1861-1865
Civil War

1865
• President Lincoln is killed.
• The Thirteenth Amendment ends slavery.

133

PEOPLE TO KNOW

Richard Allen
Patty Cannon
Thomas Garrett
Absalom Jones
Warner Mifflin
Mary Ann Shadd
Peter Spencer
Harriet Tubman

PLACES TO LOCATE

Reliance
Nanticoke River

WORDS TO UNDERSTAND

abolish
abolitionist
editor
rescue

By the year 1790 there were about 9,000 slaves in Delaware.

The men and women worked from sunup to sundown. They usually worked six days a week.

Working as a Slave

After the American Revolution, the states north of Delaware passed laws to end slavery. Pennsylvania became a free state, but Delaware and Maryland did not.

Most of the farms in Delaware were fairly small, so only a few farmers had slaves to do the work. A farmer might use a man to help with the heavy chores like plowing, weeding, and harvesting crops. He might need help caring for the oxen and horses. A slave woman might wash and iron clothes and cook as well as work in the fields.

The slaves got no money for their hard work. They lived in small houses and ate the cheapest foods. They were given clothes once or twice a year. Slaves who worked outdoors in the fields usually got Sundays off. Women who worked in the house still cooked dinner and cleaned up on Sundays before getting some time off.

Some masters were kind, but some were not. A master could beat his slaves or treat them however he wished because the slave was the master's property. The slave belonged to the master as long as he or she lived. All the children born to the slaves also belonged to the master.

Abolitionists

Even though there were many slaves in Delaware, some white people thought slavery was wrong. These people wanted to *abolish*, or end, slavery. The people were called *abolitionists.* Abolitionists urged slave owners to free their slaves. They also asked government leaders to pass a law to end slavery.

Most abolitionists were very religious. Slavery went against their idea of how God wants people to get along with one another. The Quakers and the Methodists were two religious groups that were against slavery.

The abolitionists had some success. Slavery almost disappeared in many parts of Delaware. John Dickinson, the largest land owner in Kent County, freed his slaves. Caesar Rodney put in his will that his slaves were to be freed when he died. Some masters agreed to free slaves who did extra work to buy their freedom. But slavery did not die out. Slaves still worked for masters.

This ad was placed by abolitionists. They wanted to tell other people how wrong slavery was.

What do these words mean? How would a person treat a brother?

Delaware in the Civil War

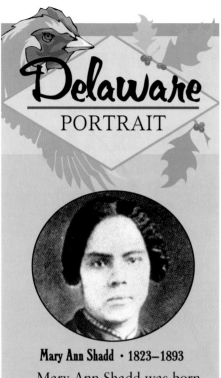
Mary Ann Shadd • 1823–1893

Mary Ann Shadd was born into a free black family in Wilmington. Her father and mother were black, but they were not slaves.

Mary Ann went to a Quaker school. When she was 16 years old, she taught in a Quaker school for black children in Wilmington. She moved to Canada and taught there, too. She loved helping young black students learn to rely on themselves and work hard.

Mary Ann Shadd believed that blacks would be better off if they moved to other places such as Canada. She started a newspaper for blacks. She was the first female *editor* of a newspaper in North America. Later, Mary Ann Shadd earned a law degree.

Warner Mifflin Frees His Slaves

Warner Mifflin was a Quaker farmer in Kent County. His family owned slaves, but he believed that slavery was wrong. He freed his slaves. He also urged other slave holders to free their slaves. Many people saw that Warner Mifflin was right. They freed their slaves, too.

Warner Mifflin traveled to other states to spread his message that slavery was wrong. He founded Delaware's first abolition society. He was one of America's first abolitionist leaders.

Free Blacks

After a while, there were more free blacks in Delaware than slaves. Most of them had little education or money and worked on farms. Some, however, had learned skills that helped them get jobs as carpenters, blacksmiths, and stable hands who took care of animals. Some free blacks owned stores. A black woman in Wilmington owned a store that was the first to sell ice cream.

Richard Allen

Richard Allen was a slave. He was owned by a farmer whom Richard described as "a good master." Despite his master's kindness, Richard longed to be free. "Slavery is a bitter pill, even though we had a good master," he said. When the master needed money, Richard's mother and three of his five brothers and sisters were sold.

Later, Richard was able to buy his freedom. He learned to read and became a minister. He moved to Philadelphia and started the African Methodist Episcopal Church.

Richard Allen bought his freedom and became a minister.

Absalom Jones

When Absalom Jones was young, he taught himself to read out of the Bible. When he was 16 years old, he was sold to a store owner in Philadelphia. He worked during the day and went to a Quaker school for blacks at night. He married another slave and bought her freedom with his earnings. Jones was finally freed by his master. He became the first black bishop in Philadelphia.

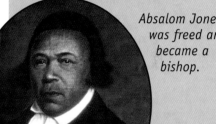

Absalom Jones was freed and became a bishop.

Peter Spencer and the Big August Quarterly

The most important black Methodist minister in Delaware was Peter Spencer. He started the Union Church of Africans in Wilmington. He also started churches in other Delaware towns and in other states.

Every August Peter Spencer's church held a meeting for all the churches he had started. Black Methodists from the whole region came to Wilmington for the meeting. It was called the Big August Quarterly.

On the day of the meeting, the streets around the church were packed with hundreds of people, both slave and free. They gathered together to pray, to hear preaching, to sing, and to see old friends. People sold food on the streets and singing groups entertained the crowd. It was a big celebration.

New Laws

For a while it appeared that slavery might die out. But slavery did not die. When some slaves in Virginia killed their master, many white people became frightened. Delaware's leaders passed a law that said free black people could not own guns. They were not allowed to meet together in groups at night.

What do you think?

Why do you think government leaders did not want blacks to own guns or meet with each other at night?

Patty Cannon and Her Gang

Delaware's free blacks could not always count on staying free. They might be captured by kidnappers and sold into slavery again.

Patty Cannon and her gang captured free blacks, tied them up, and put them in her cellar. When it was dark, the kidnappers put their captives in a boat and took them down the Nanticoke River to the Chesapeake Bay. From there the captives were taken to Virginia. Slaves there could be sold at high prices.

Patty lived in the town of Reliance. It was on the Delaware-Maryland border. If a sheriff from one state came to arrest her for kidnapping, Patty quickly moved across the border to safety. Finally, this evil woman was put in jail. She could never again kidnap people and sell them for money.

Who was kidnapped? Where and when was he stolen? How old was he?

S. WIILLAMS, Secretary.
March 16—3t

Look out for the Kidnappers.

A FREE NEGRO MAN, named Solomon Sharp, sometimes called Solomon Atkins, was kidnapped by persons unknown, from the house of William D. Atkins, in Indian River hundred, Sussex county, Delaware, on the night of the 22d of February. The said Solomon is the son of Rosannah Chippy, is aged about 22 years, about 5 feet 7 inches high and well made, light com[plexion] for a negro, has b[een]...

The Delaware Adventure

The Underground Railroad

If slaves could escape to a free state like Pennsylvania, they would be free. It was scary to run away. Runaways had to hide from masters who chased them on horses. Slaves masters used dogs to track the scent of escaped slaves.

Runaways traveled mostly at night so they would not be seen. They used the moon and stars to show them the way. They said they followed the North Star to freedom.

How did they do it? The answer is called the Underground Railroad. It was not a real railroad with train engines and cars. It wasn't even underground. The Underground Railroad was a secret way of helping slaves escape.

On the Underground Railroad, white people and free blacks gave the runaways food and places to hide. They helped slaves find the safest ways to travel. Words like "conductor" and "station" were used to hide the real purpose of the Underground Railroad.

Secret Words of the Underground Railroad

- Slaves were called "freight."
- Escape routes were called "lines."
- Those who helped the slaves move safely were "conductors."
- Safe places to spend the night were called "stations."
- Leaders were called "station masters."

Thomas Garrett Helps Slaves Escape

Thomas Garrett was a Quaker in Wilmington. Like his friend Harriet Tubman, he helped many slaves escape. He often kept runaway slaves in his house. When the sheriff's men were around, Garrett put the runaways in a wagon and covered them with hay. Then his driver took the wagon up the road and into Pennsylvania.

One time Thomas Garrett and another abolitionist were caught helping a slave woman and her children escape. Since helping slaves escape was against the law, Garrett had to pay a fine of over $5,000. At Garrett's trial, the judge said, "Thomas, I hope you will never be caught at this business again."

Garrett replied, "Friend, I haven't a dollar in the world, but if thee knows a fugitive who needs a breakfast, send him to me." Even though the fine took almost all of his money, Garrett vowed to keep helping slaves find freedom.

Thomas Garrett helped about 2,700 slaves escape to freedom. After the Civil War, the black people in Wilmington wanted to thank Garrett for all of his brave work. They had a big parade in his honor.

Thomas Garrett spent his life and most of his money helping slaves escape. He was one of the great station masters on the Underground Railroad.

Activity

The Underground Railroad

Leaders of the Underground Railroad had to work together to help the slaves escape. This is a letter Thomas Garrett wrote to abolitionist leaders in Philadelphia.

1. What two ways of transportation were the slaves using?

2. Pretend you lived then. Write a short letter explaining how you are sending runaway slaves to safety.

> I propose sending tomorrow morning by steamboat a woman and child. She has been away from . . . her master for five months.
>
> Those four I wrote thee about arrived safe up in the neighborhood [in Pennsylvania]. Harriet Tubman followed after in the stage yesterday. I shall expect five more from the same neighborhood next trip.
>
> Thomas Garrett
> May 11, 1856

The Delaware Adventure

Harriet Tubman

The most famous runaway slave was Harriet Tubman. As a young girl, she was hired out to do hard work on different farms. Once she had to wade into cold water and take dead animals out of traps. She hated that work.

When she was 24 years old, she married John Tubman, a free black man. Five years later she escaped from her master's house on Maryland's Eastern Shore. She hid by day and traveled by night. She used the North Star as her guide.

Harriet traveled through Delaware, a slave state, to the free state of Pennsylvania. Once she was free, she went back to Maryland to *rescue* other members of her family. After a while, she went back and forth many more times to lead about 300 other slaves to freedom. Sometimes she dressed as an old man or a bent-over old woman to avoid being captured.

 MEMORY MASTER

1. Why did abolitionists work to free slaves?
2. Why did Patty Cannon capture free black people?
3. What did Harriet Tubman do to help slaves?
4. What did Thomas Garrett do to help slaves?

"I looked at my hands to see if I was the same person now I was free. There was such a glory through the trees and over the hills, and I felt like I was in heaven."
—Harriet Tubman

PEOPLE TO KNOW

Lammot du Pont
Abraham Lincoln
William Owen
Anna Semple

PLACES TO LOCATE

Canada
South Carolina
Gettysburg
Pea Patch Island

WORDS TO UNDERSTAND

emancipate
fugitive
miserable
rebellion
regiment
secede

The Fugitive Slave Law

Slave masters worked to get a new law passed that would make it harder for slaves to escape. The law was called the Fugitive Slave Law. A *fugitive* is a person who is running away or trying to escape. The law said that escaped slaves had to be returned to their masters even if they had already made it safely to free states.

An escaped slave was no longer safe in Pennsylvania or anywhere in the United States. The only safe place to go was all the way to Canada. Slavery was not allowed there.

Slavery in the West

As more Americans moved west, new states were being formed. Would these new states allow slavery? People in the North said "No!" People in the South said "Yes!"

Can you see a balance between the number of slave states and free states? Can you find Delaware on the map? Was it a free state or a slave state?

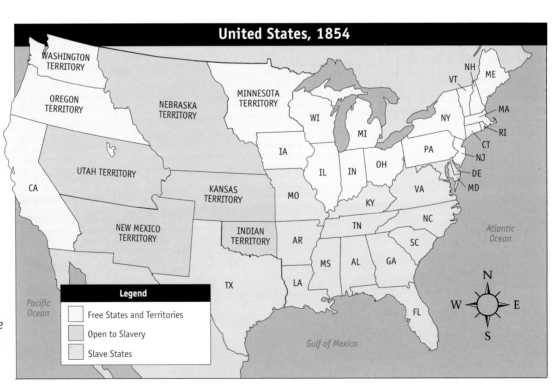

United States, 1854

Legend
- Free States and Territories
- Open to Slavery
- Slave States

New Territories Vote on Slavery

Black people, even those who were free, were usually not allowed to vote. They hoped that slavery would not spread into any new states. Then government leaders passed laws that said the people in the new territories could vote on whether or not they wanted to allow slavery.

The Election of 1860

Most of the people who lived in the northern part of the United States were against slavery. Most of the people who lived in the southern part of the country wanted to be able to own slaves. In Delaware, however, there were people with strong views on both sides. Some people in Delaware owned slaves. Others were abolitionists. Delaware was caught in the middle between the North and South.

In 1860, American voters had to choose a new president of the United States. There were four men who wanted to be elected as president. Only one was against slavery. His name was Abraham Lincoln, and he was from Illinois. Lincoln lost the election in Delaware. However, he won the vote of the northern states and was elected president of the country.

President Lincoln was still very worried about slavery. He did not think it was right. He also did not think the country would be strong if there were both slave and free states. Was Lincoln right?

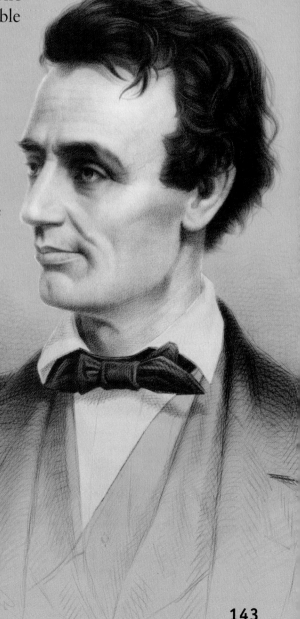

When Lincoln won the election, he did not know he would have to lead the country during a horrible war between the states.

Delaware Population in 1860

2,000 slaves

20,000 free blacks

90,000 whites

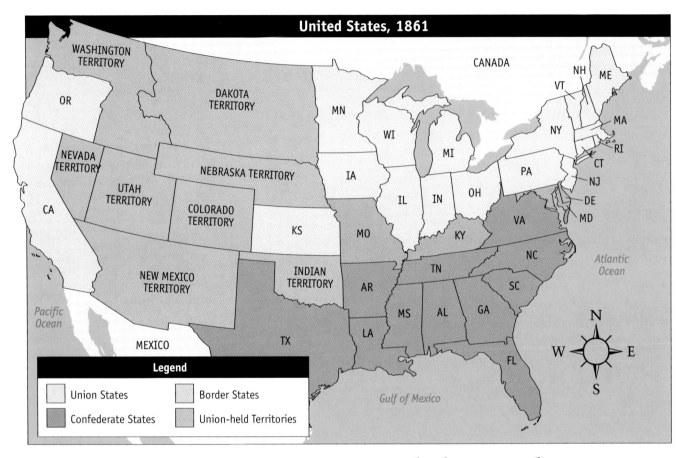

United States, 1861

WASHINGTON TERRITORY

OR

DAKOTA TERRITORY

MN

CANADA

NH   ME

VT

NY

MA

RI

CT

NEVADA TERRITORY

NEBRASKA TERRITORY

WI

MI

PA

NJ

CA

UTAH TERRITORY

IA

IL

IN

OH

DE

MD

COLORADO TERRITORY

KS

MO

VA

KY

NC

NEW MEXICO TERRITORY

INDIAN TERRITORY

AR

TN

SC

Atlantic Ocean

Pacific Ocean

MEXICO

TX

LA

MS

AL

GA

N

W   E

S

FL

Gulf of Mexico

Legend

Union States	Border States
Confederate States	Union-held Territories

The border states were part of the Union, but people there still owned slaves. Can you find Delaware on the map? What are the four border states?

Secession and the Border States

The leaders of the Southern States were very angry when Lincoln became president. South Carolina **seceded** from the Union. To secede is to break away, or to leave. Soon other Southern States did the same. They created a new country called the Confederate States of America, or the Confederacy. The states that stayed in the United States were called the Union.

Most of the slave states joined the Confederacy, but not all. Delaware, Maryland, Kentucky, and Missouri were slave states, but they stayed in the United States. They were called the border states.

President Lincoln said that no state had the right to leave the United States. He said that the United States was "one nation indivisible." Indivisible means that it cannot be divided. That is what we say in the Pledge of Allegiance.

The Delaware Adventure

Delaware Stays with the Union

Some men from the South came to Dover to ask Delaware's government leaders to join the Confederacy. The leaders replied that the people of Delaware "are now, as they ever have been, loyal to the Union; and that Delaware was the first to adopt, so she will be the last to abandon the Federal Constitution."

Attack on Fort Sumter

Fort Sumter was a United States fort. It was on an island in the harbor of Charleston, South Carolina. South Carolina had left the Union and was part of the Confederacy. The Confederates did not want U.S. soldiers in the fort. They fired cannons at the fort, and the soldiers inside finally agreed to leave. The flag of the United States was taken down from the flag pole. In its place, the flag of the Confederate States flew in the wind.

President Lincoln said that the Confederates were rebels. He called on the people of the United States to raise an army to put down the *rebellion.* A rebellion is a fight against your own government.

Inside Fort Sumter, Union soldiers loaded heavy cannonballs into cannons. Outside the fort, Confederates also fired cannons. Luckily, no one was killed in the short battle.

DE

South Carolina

• Fort Sumter

Delaware in the Civil War

More soldiers died fighting in the Civil War than in any other war in American history.

Confederate Soldiers

About 500 Delaware men joined the Confederate army.

Sometimes brothers fought on opposite sides. In one Delaware family there were four brothers. Two fought for the Union and two fought for the Confederates.

A civil war is a war between two groups in the same country. The Civil War lasted four years. The United States fought to keep the Union together. The Confederates fought to become a separate country.

None of the battles of the Civil War were fought in Delaware, but several came close. Most people in Delaware supported President Lincoln's ideas of keeping the Union together. Some people in Delaware, however, thought the Confederate States should be allowed to leave the Union. They wanted the Confederate States to win the war.

The people of Wilmington met together and gave speeches about how they could support the Union. They tried to get men to join the army. Many people went to the railroad station to cheer for the soldiers as they left the city.

Later in the war, a woman named Anna Semple started a hospital for wounded soldiers. Many women signed up to be nurses. They raised money for the hospital by making and selling quilts and pies.

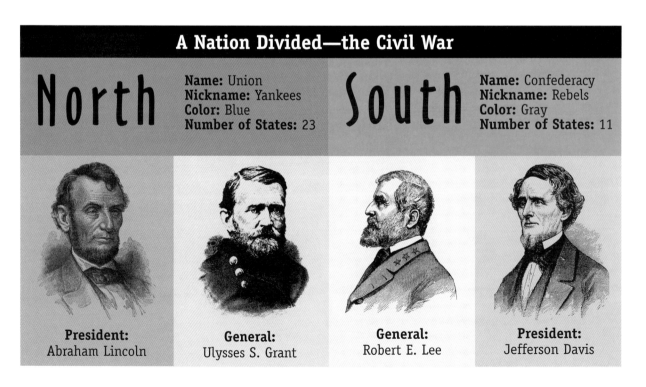

A Nation Divided—the Civil War

North
Name: Union
Nickname: Yankees
Color: Blue
Number of States: 23

South
Name: Confederacy
Nickname: Rebels
Color: Gray
Number of States: 11

President: Abraham Lincoln

General: Ulysses S. Grant

General: Robert E. Lee

President: Jefferson Davis

Delaware's Soldiers

Delaware sent over 13,000 soldiers into the Union army. Many of them fought in the largest battles of the war.

Fighting in battles was hard, but soldiers did not fight all the time. They marched from place to place. They set up camp and stayed there for a time. Then they moved on and set up another camp. Usually the soldiers slept in tents. In the winter they sometimes built small log cabins to keep out the cold and snow.

A Heavy Load

Since the soldiers marched a lot, they could not carry many things with them. They usually carried their rifles, bullets, and gunpowder. Soldiers also carried food, water, and a bedroll. Some soldiers carried books, paper, and playing cards.

Life in Camp

Soldiers spent most of their time in camp. They drilled and learned how to march. Some soldiers played cards in their spare time. Others played games such as baseball. Many soldiers played fiddles or flutes. The soldiers missed their homes. They wrote letters to their families and friends.

Posters tried to talk men into joining the war. What does the poster say the soldiers will get if they join the war?

A Union soldier dreams of a welcome home by his wife and children.

A Miserable Time

Being a soldier could be *miserable.* Can you imagine walking through mud or rivers while carrying a heavy pack on your back? Imagine the bugs and mosquitoes buzzing around as you try to sleep. It got very hot in the summer, and soldiers wore heavy uniforms. Winters were very cold, rainy, and snowy.

Many soldiers got sick and died. Soldiers often died from wounds and diseases that are easily treated today. More soldiers died from sickness than from wounds on the battlefield.

Activity

Hardly Worth Eating

Many soldiers ate hardtack during the Civil War. It was a hard cracker that would not spoil or go bad. It was called hardtack because it was very hard. A soldier once wrote home that he bit into his hardtack and found something soft. It was a nail! Of course, that was just a joke, but the story hints that hardtack was very hard to bite and chew.

With the help of an adult, you can make your own hardtack. Here is the recipe:

Mix 2 cups of flour, 1 cup of water, and a pinch of salt into a dough. Drop mounds of dough on a cookie sheet and flatten them out. Then use a fork or a big nail to poke holes in the dough. Be sure not to leave the nail in the dough!

Bake at 375 degrees for one hour. You've got hardtack!

Black Soldiers

African American men were eager to fight against the Confederates. The United States Army welcomed blacks, but segregated them into all-black *regiments.*

No black regiment was formed in Delaware. The men had to go to another state to join the army. Most joined regiments in Pennsylvania. About 1,000 black men from Delaware served in the army.

William Owen

William Owen was a free black man from Milford. He was 39 years old when he decided to enlist. Most soldiers were only half his age. William Owen walked all the way to Massachusetts to join the army. His regiment was the Massachusetts 54th, which became famous for great bravery.

This painting is titled "Come and Join Us Brothers." The painting was used to get African American men to fight for the Union.

This man is playing the role of William Owen.

Freeing the Slaves

The war cost many lives. President Lincoln believed that the best way to end the war was to free the slaves. He admired Delaware for the little state's stand for the Union. He chose Delaware to be part of an experiment. He offered to pay slave masters to free their slaves.

The plan did not work. Too many people were against it. President Lincoln gave up his experiment and decided instead to free all the slaves in the Confederacy.

President Lincoln wrote a document called the Emancipation Proclamation. To *emancipate* means to set free. The Emancipation Proclamation only tried to free slaves in the Confederacy. It did not free the slaves in Delaware or in the other loyal border states.

The Emancipation Proclamation freed slaves in the states that were not loyal to the union. Most slave owners, however, ignored the proclamation.

Wilmington Makes War Supplies

Wilmington was Delaware's main manufacturing city. Its factories kept busy filling orders for the army and the navy. Workers made leather belts, shoes, and holsters for soldiers' guns. They also made harnesses for horses that pulled supply wagons. Workers made army wagons. A company made material for tents and uniforms.

Shipbuilders supplied all kinds of ships and boats to the Union. The *Saugus* was one of four ships built in Wilmington. Over 200 men built the *Saugus*. It was protected by sheets of iron on its sides. A cannon on the ship could turn around to fire in any direction.

The Du Pont Powder Yards

During wartime, the most important industry in Delaware was the Du Pont Company. It was the largest maker of black powder in the United States. Black powder was used as an explosive. It was also used as gunpowder.

Saltpeter was a mineral important for making gunpowder. There was no saltpeter in the United States. The best place to buy it was in England. At the start of the war, Lammot du Pont went to England as fast as he could to buy saltpeter for his family's company. He made secret deals and bought all the saltpeter he could get. He made sure that the Union would have the gunpowder it needed.

People were afraid that the Confederates would try to blow up the company's buildings on the Brandywine River. Soldiers were sent to guard the yard.

Lammot du Pont made sure the United States had all the gunpowder it needed.

You can learn a lot about how gunpowder was made at the Hagley Museum. What kind of transportation do you see in this picture of the powder yards?

PA

NJ

MD

DE

VA

NC

• Gettysburg

The Battle of Gettysburg

The Union met the Confederates at the little town of Gettysburg, Pennsylvania. The largest battle of the Civil War was fought there. It lasted three days. Over 20,000 men died on each side.

On the third day of the battle, the Confederates came across a field and attacked the Union army. Their attack is known as Pickett's Charge. Troops from Delaware stood at the center of the Union line of soldiers and helped to push the Confederates back. It was a horrible battle. After it was over, the Confederate army marched back to Virginia and never invaded the North again.

When news of the Union victory reached Delaware, the whole state celebrated. People hung flags on houses and stores. Church bells rang. Those who had wanted the Confederacy to win kept silent.

Fort Delaware

The Union took many prisoners during the Battle of Gettysburg. The prisoners were sent to Fort Delaware. At first, the prisoners were kept in the fort. Then the prison got too crowded, so men were put in tents on the island's swampy ground. Except for a few very strong swimmers, no one escaped.

The prison was a crowded, miserable place. Thousands of the prisoners died of wounds or from sickness. Smallpox killed hundreds of soldiers. Those who lived spent their time swatting mosquitoes in summer and shivering with cold in winter.

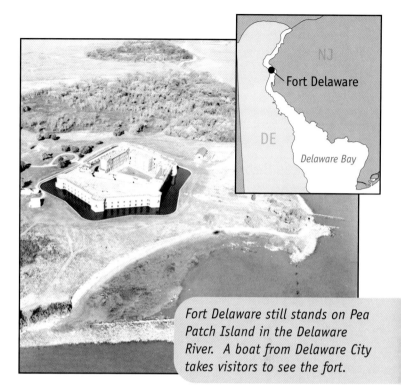

Fort Delaware still stands on Pea Patch Island in the Delaware River. A boat from Delaware City takes visitors to see the fort.

Cameras—a New Invention

Photography was very new in the Civil War years. For the first time, people could see pictures of battlefields, camps, and soldiers. The pictures were put in magazines and newspapers.

Here are photographs of two brothers, Rodman and Linton Smith. They were soldiers from Delaware. Many soldiers had their pictures taken wearing their new uniforms before they went off to war. Like most soldiers, the Smith brothers sent letters to tell the folks back home what army life was like.

Linton Smith

S. Rodman Smith

2 MEMORY MASTER

1. How did the Fugitive Slave Law affect runaway slaves?
2. What were the names of the two sides during the Civil War?
3. Which side in the war did most Delaware soldiers join?
4. What did Delaware's factories make for the war?

PEOPLE TO KNOW

John Wilkes Booth
Sarah Evans
Abraham Lincoln

WORDS TO UNDERSTAND

Reconstruction

The War Ends

When spring came in 1865, the Union army had nearly surrounded the Confederate army in Virginia. The Confederates surrendered. The war was finally over.

Everyone in the North was happy that the long war was over. The soldiers would soon be coming home. All the states were one country again. All the slaves in the country would soon be freed. There were parades all over the North.

The states in the South, of course, were not happy. Many of the battles had been fought on their ground. Roads and railroads had been ruined. Bridges had been blown up. Whole cities had been burned. Farms had been left to turn to weeds. Plantation owners knew it would not be long until slavery would end. The Emancipation Proclamation had freed the slaves in the South. Plantation owners would have to start paying their workers. No one would repay them for the cost they had paid to buy the slaves. Life was about to change for everyone.

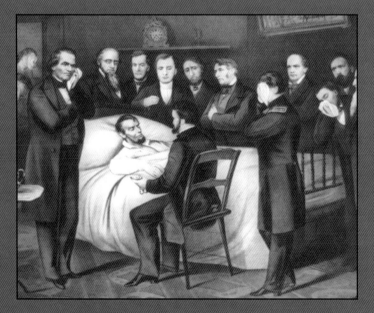

President Lincoln Is Shot

A few days after the end of the war, a terrible thing happened. President Lincoln and his wife, Mary, were watching a play in a theater in Washington, D.C. A Confederate actor named John Wilkes Booth shot President Lincoln. Lincoln died early the next morning.

The whole country mourned for the president. He had worked to put the country back together again. Now he would no longer lead it in a time of peace.

Reconstruction

Before he died, President Lincoln had told the country that they should not try to punish the people in the South. Instead, they should put away their bad feelings and try to give the people in the South a chance to rebuild their cities and their lives. Lincoln had talked about rebuilding, or *Reconstruction,* of the South. He said:

> *With malice toward none; with charity for all, . . . let us strive on to finish the work we are in; to bind up the nation's wounds and achieve a lasting peace. . . .*

Free at Last

Reconstruction meant more than rebuilding land. People's lives had to be rebuilt, too. The United States added a new amendment to the U.S. Constitution. The Thirteenth Amendment abolished slavery everywhere in the United States. All of Delaware's slaves were free.

Government leaders wanted to do more than just end slavery. They wanted to give black people the same rights that white people had. First, they wanted to give black men the right to vote. Second, they wanted to provide education for all black people in the South.

What do you think?

- What does the word "malice" mean? Do people usually feel malice towards the enemy in a time of war?

- How hard is it to feel "charity," or kindness, towards someone who has harmed you?

- Do you think charity is important?

Many former slaves left the South and went north to find jobs. They were overjoyed to start a life of freedom.

Education

It had been against the law to teach slaves to read or write. Masters had feared that their slaves would read about the abolitionists and make plans to escape. Now the former slaves were eager to learn. Many free blacks had not learned to read, either. They wanted to go to school.

The Freedmen's Bureau

The government created an agency called the Freedmen's Bureau to help the freed slaves. The Freedmen's Bureau hired people who worked to find jobs, homes, food, clothes, and medical help for blacks. The Freedmen's Bureau also worked hard to set up schools for former slaves of all ages.

In Wilmington, people raised money to build schools for blacks. Blacks helped to build the schools. The group hired teachers. The teachers included blacks and whites, men and women. Their students included whole families, fathers, mothers, grandparents, and children. They were all eager to learn.

What do you think?

What would it be like to know that you could go to school for the first time? What would you most want to learn about?

Blocksoms Colored School taught children of all ages. Even parents could go to school.

Hard Beginnings

Some white people were against helping black people study in school. Life for the teachers was not easy. One school was burned, but it was quickly rebuilt. It was hard to keep the schools going because they had so little money.

Delaware created separate public schools for black children. The struggle to end slavery was over, but black students and white students were kept separate from each other.

What do you think?

Talk with your class about the meaning of equality. How does education help people be more equal?

Sarah Evans Teaches School

One of the teachers who came to Delaware to teach in a school for black people was Sarah Evans. Sarah Evans was a young black woman from Philadelphia. She was sent to teach in Georgetown. She lived there with a black minister and his family.

One night, when the minister and his family were not at home, a gang of bullies came to the house. They did not want black people to go to school. They threw stones at the house and yelled threats against Sarah.

Sarah was very afraid. She managed to escape from the house and went to the sheriff's house, but he was not home. She went to the house of a friend, who let her hide in a barn. The next day Sarah went home to Philadelphia and did not come back.

Sarah's school may have looked like this one.

❸ MEMORY MASTER

1. What happened to President Lincoln just after the war ended?
2. What was Reconstruction?
3. What did the Freedmen's Bureau do?
4. What problems did black teachers and students face?

From There to Here

Slavery divided the United States into the North and the South. Slavery also divided Delaware because it was on the border between the two sides. Most of Delaware's black people were free, but some were slaves. Abolitionists worked to end slavery and help slaves escape.

When the South seceded from the Union, Delaware remained loyal to the United States. Many Delaware men fought for the Union army in the Civil War. After the Civil War ended, the Thirteenth Amendment to the U.S. Constitution made slavery illegal in the United States. All people in Delaware became free.

What Do You Remember?

1. Why was Delaware so split on the issue of slavery?
2. What did abolitionists think about slavery?
3. How did abolitionists help slaves?
4. What part did Delaware play in the Civil War?
5. What did the Emancipation Proclamation do?
6. What happened to President Lincoln just after the Civil War ended?

Geography 🌍 Tie-In

Look at a map that shows Dorchester County, Maryland, where Harriet Tubman grew up. Then find the states of Delaware and Pennsylvania. Find the towns and rivers between Tubman's home in Maryland and Philadelphia.

Now write a short story about how Harriet Tubman and other slaves might have escaped. Use places from the map in your story.

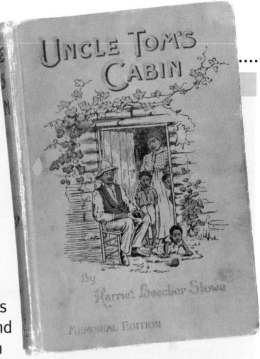

Activity

The Power of a Book

Harriet Beecher Stowe was an abolitionist in Ohio. She felt it was her duty to help the slaves, so she wrote a book called *Uncle Tom's Cabin*. The book was not written for children. It told about the horrible lives of some slaves in the South and about their efforts to escape. It was very sad, but it was also very exciting. Many people in the North read the book and worked harder to end slavery.

With your class, act out the part of the book where Eliza, a young slave mother, hears her master's wife telling someone that she must sell Eliza's son and old Uncle Tom in order to pay some debts. Eliza's son is a clever five-year-old boy who sings and dances. She cannot bear to part with him.

When it gets dark, Eliza takes her son so he won't be sold to another master. They run. They are frightened. They hear the master coming after them with barking dogs. They finally get to the Ohio River and jump from one ice block to another to cross into Ohio. Ohio is a free state. Eliza and her son are rescued by a kind Quaker family. Soon Eliza's husband, who has escaped from a different master, joins her. Old Uncle Tom, however, remains loyal to his master and does not try to escape.

Activities

Write and Draw About the Civil War

Choose one or more of these activities to learn more about life during the Civil War:

1. Read more about the attack on Fort Sumter in library books and on the Internet. Then draw a picture of the attack. Write a few sentences to tell about what is happening in your picture.

2. Pretend you are a soldier in the Civil War. Write a letter home and tell your family what your life is like.

3. Write a paragraph to explain why the Emancipation Proclamation did not free the slaves in Delaware.

Delaware in the Civil War

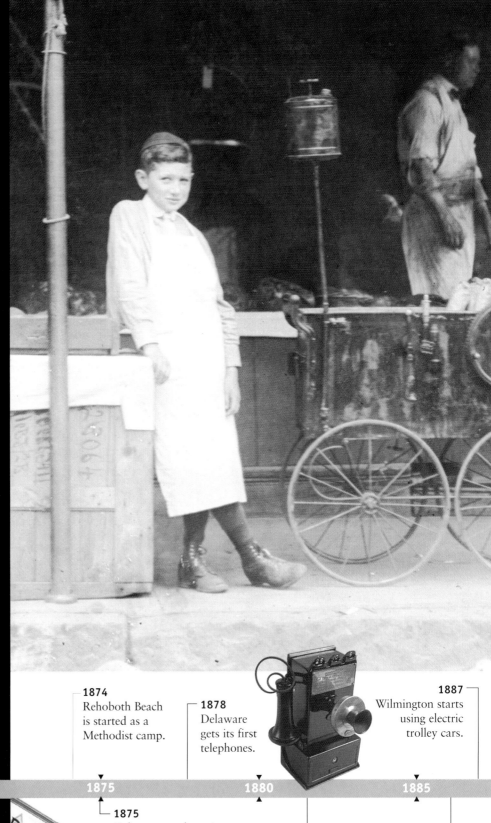

"*I ran home to tell my mother and father that I had found a job. . . . My father said, 'Good. You are becoming a man now.' I was 12, but I could feel that he was proud of me.*"

—*Leonard Covello*

Timeline of Events

1874
Rehoboth Beach is started as a Methodist camp.

1878
Delaware gets its first telephones.

1887
Wilmington starts using electric trolley cars.

1875

1880

1885

1875
Delaware produces its largest peach crop.

1882
Delaware gets electricity.

1886
The Statue of Liberty first welcomes immigrants to the United States of America.

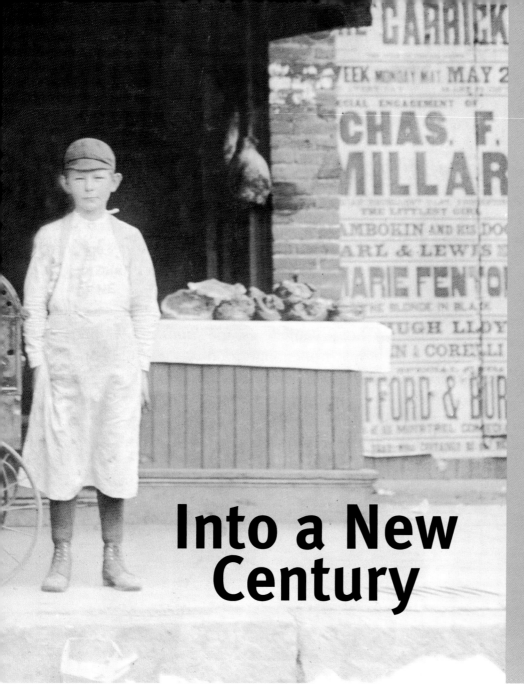

In 1910, George Bogart (on left), age 11, worked at a vegetable stand owned by his father. He earned 25 cents a week. His friend Norman Colt, age 12, also worked at the stand to earn some money of his own.

Into a New Century

1888–1889
Disease destroys most peach orchards.

1898
Delaware sells subway cars to London.

1903
Delaware begins to pave streets.

1905
Delaware passes a law to protect children who work.

1890   1895   1900   1905

1890s
The first automobiles are made in America.

1890
Black powder explodes at the DuPont Company.

1901
• Sarah Pyle opens the Peoples Settlement to help immigrants.
• Sussex County produces more strawberries than any other county in America.

161

PEOPLE TO KNOW

Mary Babiarz
Angelo Citro
Sally Topkis
Dominic DeSabatino

PLACES TO LOCATE

Germany
Ireland
Italy
Poland
Russia
Wilmington
Ellis Island

WORDS TO UNDERSTAND

famine
immigrant

Immigrants from many countries came to America for a better life. Many did not speak English. They had different customs. How do you think they felt as they started a new life in a new country?

Coming to Delaware

Millions of *immigrants* came to the United States in the late 1800s. An immigrant is a person who moves into a new country to live. It was hard for them to leave their families and friends, but immigrants came to America to find a better life.

The Irish were the first people to come to Delaware in large numbers. Some came to escape *famine*. A famine is a time when there is not enough food to eat, and people starve. Many other people came to find good jobs. They came from Germany, Italy, and Poland. Jewish people from Russia, Poland, and Germany also came because the governments there forced them to leave their homes.

By Foot, by Wagon, by Train, by Ship

Coming to America was exciting, scary, and tiring. No matter what country people came from, they had a long journey ahead of them. They had to walk or ride in a wagon from their homes to a train station. Then trains took them to the ships that would bring them to America. Immigrant ships left from Europe's big seaports.

Most people could only afford the cheapest ticket. They had to share rooms with people they did not know. Their rooms were at the bottom of the ship near the engines. These were the hottest and noisiest rooms on the ship.

Each room had many bunk beds. The food was not very good. Some people got very seasick. Others enjoyed meeting people, playing music, and walking outside up on the deck.

Only people who had a lot of money could travel in nicer rooms that were higher up on the ship. They might even have a small window where they could look outside at the ocean and the sky.

The Top Five Reasons People Came to America

1. To escape poverty and poor living conditions.
2. To escape war.
3. To practice the religion of their choice.
4. To enjoy other freedoms of American life.
5. To join other family members.

Welcome to the United States of America

Before they got off the ships, thousands of immigrants were greeted by the Statue of Liberty. She was a gift to our country from France. The gift was to celebrate America's 100th birthday. The grand statue still welcomes people to the harbor at New York City.

Then immigrants were taken on ferry boats to a large building on Ellis Island. It was a place where immigrants had to pass a health exam. Doctors looked at the immigrants' eyes and skin and watched to see if they could walk up the stairs without limping or getting out of breath.

Those who were healthy could buy a train ticket to other places. If a person had a disease, he or she was put in a room away from other people so the sickness would not spread.

The Statue of Liberty in New York Harbor welcomed families from many countries.

Journey to Delaware

Ellis Island was the first stop for many immigrants.

Mary Babiarz Comes from Poland

Mary Babiarz was born in Poland to poor farmers. She had a cousin in Delaware who offered to loan her money for a ticket to America. At age 16, Mary came to America all alone. She had only $2.50 and her ticket. Her parents cried when they left her at the train.

Many years later Mary talked about what happened when she got to the ship in Germany:

They took us down below. I didn't carry a lot of bags, just what I had on and a little bag. I couldn't get on the deck because I was sick all that trip . . . all eleven days down there alone, I couldn't lift my head.

Once she got to New York, Mary was put on a train to Wilmington. When she got off at the train station, the sun had not come up yet. It was still dark.

I had an address on a piece of paper, and I showed it to the people who took care of the station. I looked all the way down the street, and it was dark . . . what am I going to do?

Then a man going to work stopped to help. Mary showed him the address, and the man walked her there.

Passengers got off ships and waited at Ellis Island until they had permission to leave. Sometimes they waited a long time. Children fell asleep by their mothers.

The Delaware Adventure

Angelo Citro Comes from Italy

Angelo Citro lived on a farm in Italy. He had no friends or family in America, but at age 19 he made plans to move across the ocean. Years later, Angelo told about his trip:

We had . . . bunk beds. There were six men in your cabin. . . . Women were in another section. . . . [To eat] you just had to wait in line, get your lunch, and then bring it back to your cabin.

Angelo had met another young man on the boat. His new friend had a brother in Wilmington. Angelo decided to go to Wilmington, too.

Some people have relatives who come after them. Some people have nobody, like me.

Immigrants who had to stay overnight slept in a large room full of bunk beds.

Sally Topkis Comes from Russia

Sally Topkis and her family had to flee from Russia because of their religion. They were Jews, and the ruler of Russia wanted to drive all of the Jews out of his country. He burned down their houses and businesses. He had his soldiers kill people who did not leave.

When the soldiers burned down her father's store, Sally and her family hid in the basement. When the soldiers left, the family left. They traveled to Germany. Sally was just a little girl about three years old, but she remembered that they had a long wait for a boat because so many people were leaving.

Life was busy on the immigrant ship. What is going on in this photograph?

① MEMORY MASTER

1. List three reasons why immigrants came to Delaware.
2. What special problems did immigrants face?

PEOPLE TO KNOW

Alfred I. du Pont
Joshua Marvil
Alden Richardson
James Robbins
John G. Townsend Jr.

PEOPLE TO KNOW

China
London, England
Paris, France
Delaware City
Dover
Laurel
Port Penn
Rehoboth Beach
Selbyville
Wilmington

PEOPLE TO KNOW

dynamite
soot

Factories produced goods, but they also made the air very dirty.

The Bad Side of Industry

After the Civil War, Wilmington was a dirty city. All the factories made the city dirty. Factories burned coal to power the steam engines that ran the machines. Tall smokestacks belched black smoke and *soot.* Soot is a fine black dust that settled over the city. Only later did people learn that black smoke and soot are bad for people's health.

The Explosion of 1890

There were other dangers too. The Du Pont Powder Yards had supplied most of the gunpowder used during the Civil War. Then the company also started making *dynamite.* Men lit the dynamite to make it explode. The explosions blew up rock and earth. This helped clear away rock that was in the way when workers needed to build a tunnel or level the land for a new railroad track.

The greatest fear at the powder yards was that the black powder and dynamite would catch fire and explode. Then it happened. Tons of powder blew up. Fifty houses were knocked down. Twelve people died. The sound of the explosion was so loud that the people of Wilmington ran into the streets in terror. There had been many explosions, but this was the worst one.

"I Was There"

Edward Cheney lived in a worker's house just outside the powder yards. His father, brother, and grandfather worked for the company. He was too young to work in the powder yards, but Edward remembered the great explosion all the rest of his life. This is what he said about it:

During the explosion of 1890, I was asleep on a settee [sofa]. The shock of the explosion threw me onto the floor. . . . George, my brother, got behind a great oak tree and he saw different objects flying by . . . there was a piece of a railroad rail driven right into a tree.

The terrible explosion shook the earth for miles and miles. Houses rocked and windows broke.

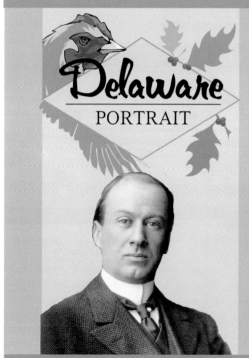

Delaware PORTRAIT

Alfred I. du Pont • 1865–1935

Alfred du Pont loved the powder yards. He grew up near them and often played with the children of the workers. Alfred's parents died when he was 12, but he stayed in his home with his older brothers and sisters.

When he grew older, Alfred went away to college. He came back to become the boss of the powder yards. Alfred liked to work with the men. He liked to get his hands dirty making black powder.

Then the company president died, and Alfred and two cousins changed things at the company. They bought other companies and hired scientists to do research on chemicals. Alfred wanted to produce more than black powder. The cousins moved the company from Hagley to Wilmington.

In later years, du Pont and his wife moved to Florida. When he died, he left his money to help crippled children and homeless people in Delaware and Florida. Today, the Alfred I. duPont Hospital for Children takes care of thousands of children from across the country and around the world.

Ships and Railroad Cars

The biggest companies in Wilmington built ships and railroad cars. The factories were all located between the Christina River and the railroad lines. This was the perfect location. The factories could use both the river and the railroad to bring in the coal, lumber, and iron they needed to make their products.

The big factories built train cars that were used on the first railroad that went all across the United States. They were even used in China. The subways of London and Paris used subway cars made in Wilmington.

Some railroad cars and ships were very plain. They were used to carry goods and large numbers of people. Other railroad cars and ships were very fancy. They had nice chairs covered with leather or velvet. They had carved woodwork and curtains on the windows.

Carpenters, ironworkers, engine builders, and painters all worked together. More than 1,000 people worked in a big factory. The noise of the machinery was very loud. Saws shrieked, big hammers pounded, and endless moving belts carried parts. The belts rattled on and on.

Leathermaking

The other big business in Wilmington was tanning leather. Tanning was long, dirty, and very smelly work. First, workers scraped animal hides to take off all the fur. Then workers soaked the skins in big vats, or tubs, of chemicals to make them soft. Finally, workers rubbed, polished, or colored the skins.

Some leather went to the railroad car and shipbuilding factories. Leather was used to cover the seats on the fancy railroad cars and steamboats. This was sturdy leather that was meant to last. Softer, thinner leather went to workers who made shoes and gloves.

Wilmington's big factories built most of the steamboats that ran on the Delaware River. They also built steamboats that ran on the Amazon River in South America.

The Peach Boom

You read about the start of the big peach orchards in an earlier chapter. Planting peach trees started in Delaware City, but soon trees were being planted everywhere in the state. Workers planted more than 5 million peach trees. People called it a peach boom.

Farmers were happy because they could make money selling fresh peaches to the people in big cities. Sellers shouted out:

> *"Here are your peaches,*
> *Your nice Delaware peaches,*
> *Your sweet Delaware peaches!"*

It took many people and millions of baskets to move the peaches from the trees to the markets. Some of the peaches were carried by ships, but even more went by train. At the height of the peach boom, the railroad had to add more trains. Delaware's peaches filled nearly a million train cars every year. That's a lot of peaches!

Joshua H. Marvil Makes Fruit Baskets

At harvest time, farmers needed baskets to hold the fruit. Some people went into business to make baskets for peaches, strawberries, and other fruits and vegetables. The biggest basket-making factory was in Laurel. It was started by Joshua Marvil. He invented a machine that made berry baskets. His company made two million baskets a year.

The Richardson and Robbins Cannery

Alden Richardson and James Robbins built the biggest cannery in Delaware. It was located in Dover. The men were tinsmiths. Tinsmiths made metal objects such as candleholders, plates, or buckets. The men decided they could add a cannery to their business. They already knew how to make tin cans.

Over the years the cannery grew. At first, all of the sorting, washing, cutting up, and cooking of the fruit was done by hand. Then large machines made the work faster and easier.

Canning Peaches

Soon there were too many peaches. To keep them from going bad, people decided to put them in cans and cook them. The peaches could then be sold and eaten all winter. The first cannery was built in Port Penn.

The End of the Peach Boom

A disease began to attack the peach trees. It was called the "yellows" because it turned the leaves of the peach tree yellow. Farmers had no way to fight the disease. A tree with the yellows died within two years.

Fruit was picked, cleaned, cut, and then cooked in metal cans.

Other Fruits and Vegetables by the Bushel

Farmers needed new crops to replace the peaches. They began to plant many other fruits and vegetables. They planted tomatoes, peas, watermelons, strawberries, and apples. These fruits and vegetables were sold fresh or canned.

Strawberries

Of all the fruits and vegetables, strawberries became the most important. Strawberry plants like sandy soil, so they grew very well in Sussex County. Soon farmers there grew more strawberries than any other place in America.

Strawberries were first sold fresh to stores in cities all along the East Coast. Railroad cars used big blocks of ice to keep strawberries fresh as they moved from the fields to the stores.

Soon there were so many strawberries that the stores couldn't sell all of them. A man had an idea. He canned strawberries to make sweet syrup. Then he used this syrup to make the first strawberry soda in America. He poured some pink syrup, a scoop of vanilla ice cream, and some soda into a glass. Soon people everywhere wanted ice cream sodas and sundaes.

Tomatoes, tomatoes, and more tomatoes. Notice the wagons and horses that brought tomatoes from the farms to the cannery. The train probably took canned tomatoes to market.

Trains Carry Freight and People

After the Civil War ended, the railroad helped Delaware grow. Railroads laid tracks to connect small towns with the big cities. The railroads made it easy for the big factories in Wilmington to ship the things they made to markets throughout the country. Farmers sent fruits and vegetables to market on the trains.

Trains carried people as well as freight. People wanted to get to other places to shop, work, or just visit friends and family. Riding on a train was the easiest and fastest way to travel. Trains also made it easier to spend a day, a week, or the whole summer at Delaware's beaches.

A Vacation Town

Rehoboth Beach was Delaware's first vacation town. It was begun as a place for a Methodist camp meeting. Before the railroad came, it was not easy to get to Rehoboth Beach. Visitors had to travel by horse and wagon or by boat.

Rehoboth Beach grew after the railroad came. The boardwalk got longer, and many hotels and restaurants were built. Soon Dewey Beach, Bethany Beach, and other seashore towns became busy vacation places.

The Rehoboth Beach Railroad brought visitors. They dressed up in their Sunday clothes to ride the train.

Rehoboth
• Beach

Do you dress like this to play at the beach?

The Delaware Adventure

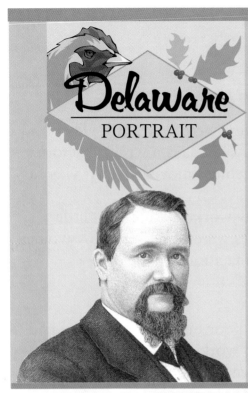

John Townsend Jr. • 1871–1964

John Townsend Jr. was born in Maryland and grew up on a farm. He loved the farm, but he saw that earning a living as a farmer was very hard. When he was a young man, he moved to Delaware.

Before telephones were invented, people sent messages over the telegraph. They used a system of short and long sounds that spelled out words. Operators tapped out the code on a telegraph machine. The sounds went quickly from place to place along wires that had been hung from pole to pole.

Townsend became a telegraph operator for the railroad. He got the messages, wrote them out, and delivered them to people.

Townsend always looked around for new ways to earn a living. He worked as a banker, sold lumber, grew fruits and vegetables to sell, and owned canneries. He bought thousands of acres of land for his fruit and vegetable fields.

Townsend was elected governor of Delaware. Later, he became a United States senator. He worked for good schools and good highways. He also worked to get women the right to vote.

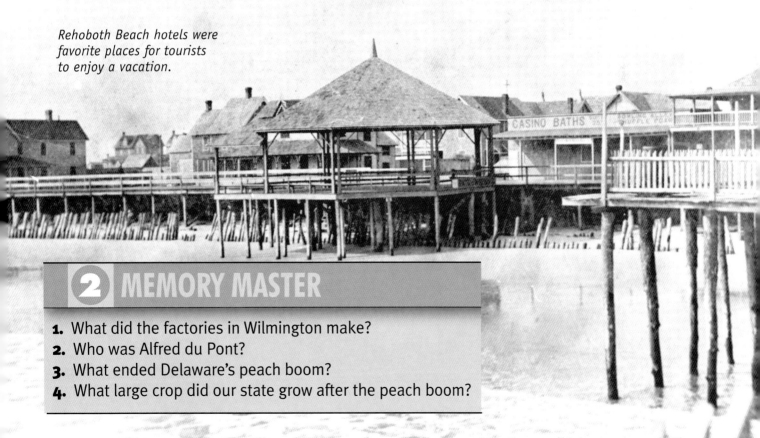

Rehoboth Beach hotels were favorite places for tourists to enjoy a vacation.

2 MEMORY MASTER

1. What did the factories in Wilmington make?
2. Who was Alfred du Pont?
3. What ended Delaware's peach boom?
4. What large crop did our state grow after the peach boom?

PEOPLE TO KNOW

Jane Addams
Mary Babiarz
Sarah Webb Pyle
Mary Ann Sorden Stuart

PLACES TO LOCATE

Greenwood
Chicago, Illinois

WORDS TO UNDERSTAND

customs
discrimination
labor unions
segregation
strike

Working in Factories

The lives of factory workers were very hard. They had to work up to 12 hours a day, six days a week. Factories were hot and noisy. The machines moved fast. It was easy to get hurt.

For all their work, factory workers were paid little money. Most factory workers were men, but many women and children also worked in factories.

Women at Work

Many women, especially poor immigrant women, had to work. Mary Babiarz had to work when she came to Delaware from Poland. It was hard for Mary because she did not have a good education or training on machines. She spoke very poor English. Mary got a job in a leather factory. The work was hard, and she did not make much money. But at least she had a job.

Workers made socks all day at the Delaware Hosiery Mill in Wilmington.

The Delaware Adventure

Women worked to make money for themselves and their families. Only the rich did not work. Some women worked in their own homes. They washed and ironed other people's clothes. They made things to sell. Many women were cooks or maids in other people's houses. A few women were schoolteachers, nurses, or clerks in stores. Some women worked in offices.

Women who worked in factories and canneries usually did not need training or education. They did "unskilled labor." These women were paid very low wages no matter how hard they worked.

Each morning, men and women came to the Bancroft Mills. They worked at machines that wove cotton thread into cloth.

Skilled Jobs for Women

A few factories began to hire women to do "skilled labor" that needed more training. Working with wood and painting were some of the skilled labor jobs. People who had this work earned a little more money than unskilled workers.

Men Strike

Harlan and Hollingsworth was the first factory in Wilmington to hire women to do skilled jobs. The bosses hired women to paint the insides of ships. This made male painters angry because the women got the work that the men had done on rainy days when they could not work outside. The men said that they would *strike.* This means they would all stop working at the same time so the company would have to give them what they wanted. The company, however, said to go ahead and strike. The company would just hire more women.

The men backed down and kept working. Soon Harlan and Hollingsworth had women painting and sewing. The men got used to having women doing skilled work in the factory. Soon other factories hired women to do skilled work.

Children at Work

Very young children pick the stems off strawberries at Johnson's Farm.

Children often had to work to help their families pay rent and buy food. Children in Delaware worked outdoors and indoors. During the summer, children worked on farms and in canneries.

Other children and teenagers worked all year. Some worked in factories doing hard, dirty work. Some polished shoes or sold newspapers on street corners.

Children who worked had no time to go to school. Many barely knew how to read and write. They did not know much arithmetic. This meant they usually could not get good jobs when they got older.

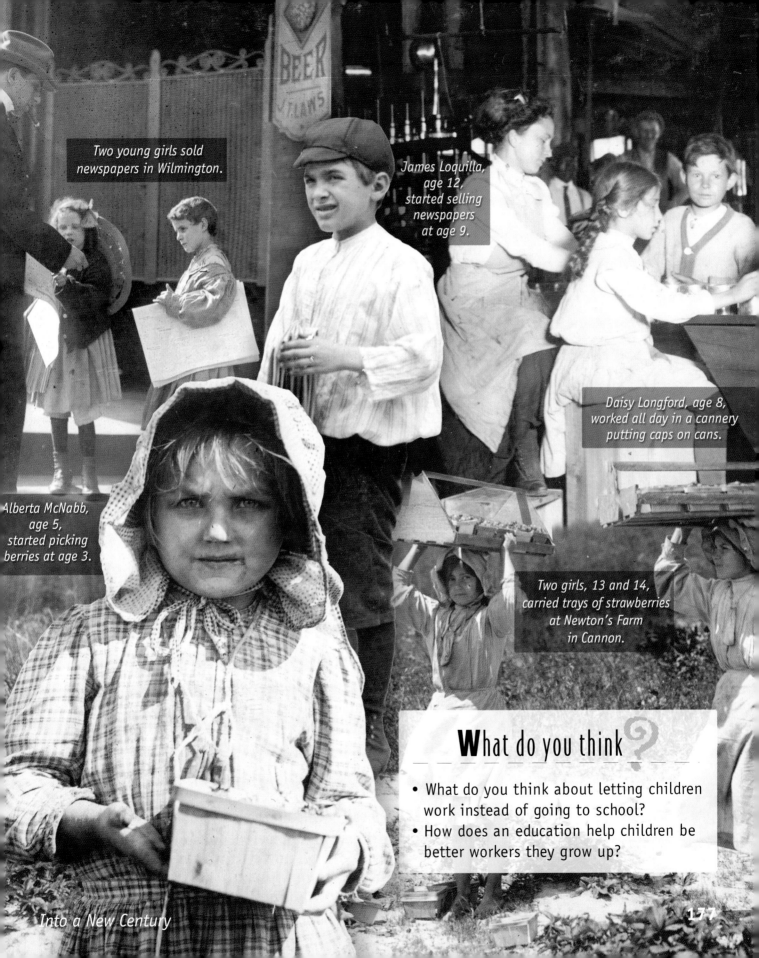

Two young girls sold newspapers in Wilmington.

James Loquilla, age 12, started selling newspapers at age 9.

Alberta McNabb, age 5, started picking berries at age 3.

Daisy Longford, age 8, worked all day in a cannery putting caps on cans.

Two girls, 13 and 14, carried trays of strawberries at Newton's Farm in Cannon.

What do you think ?

- What do you think about letting children work instead of going to school?
- How does an education help children be better workers they grow up?

Into a New Century

Working for Change

Many workers believed factory owners did not treat them fairly. They thought factories were often unsafe and unhealthy. They thought wages were too low.

The workers began to fight for change. They went on strike until they got more money or a safer work space. These workers formed groups called **labor unions.** The unions fought for workers' rights.

In Wilmington, factory workers often went on strike. They thought it was unfair when their wages were cut or they had to do more work in the same amount of time.

Workers hoped that if they refused to work, the bosses would make things better. Going on strike was risky. A person did not get paid while on strike. Strikers could lose their jobs. Going on strike did not always get bosses to pay more or make a factory safer.

Leather Workers Strike

Many workers in Wilmington joined a national union called the Knights of Labor. The Knights of Labor put together the biggest strike yet in Wilmington. The strike was in the leather factories. Workers walked out of the factories and said they would not go back until they got better pay.

The strike lasted for many months. The owners would not agree to pay workers more money. Instead, they hired new workers who would work for less money.

Finally, some of the old workers agreed to go back to work. They decided that their low pay was better than no pay at all. The big strike had failed.

What do you think?

- Should the bosses have paid the workers more money?
- Was it fair that men and women had to work in unsafe places?

Celebrating Labor Day

Even though workers were not paid very much, they were proud of their work. In cities all across the country, factory workers began to hold a special event every September. They called it Labor Day.

Each year on Labor Day, thousands of workers marched in parades that had bands and floats. People gave speeches in the parks. There was often a picnic and a dance. Later, the U.S. government made Labor Day a holiday.

Children march in a Labor Day Parade. They wear banners written in several languages. The banners read "Abolish Child Slavery." What did this mean?

Protecting Women and Children

Some people wanted to help children who worked. They wanted the government to pass laws that would make sure children did not get hurt or sick from working in factories. They wanted children to have the chance to go to school.

Lawmakers in Delaware passed a law that helped children who worked in factories. The law said that children under age 14 could not work in factories. They had to go to school. Children from 14 to 16 could work only 54 hours a week. Children over 16 could work as long as adults did.

This law did not help children who worked on farms or in canneries. They still worked all summer for as many hours as their parents needed them to.

Women who worked also needed help. They needed clean work areas. They needed to work fewer hours so they could take care of their families at home. Lawmakers agreed. They passed laws that helped women who worked in factories.

Linking the Past to the Present

Today, many adults work 8 hours a day, 5 days a week. How many total hours per week do they work? How does this compare to the number of hours the old laws said children aged 14 to 16 could work in factories?

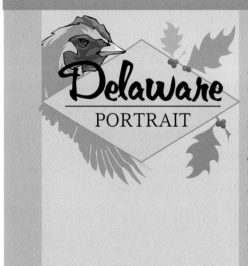

Delaware PORTRAIT

Mary Ann Sorden Stuart • 1828–1893

Mary Ann Stuart lived in Greenwood. When her husband died, she had five young children. She needed to work to take care of her family, so she went into business.

Mary Ann learned that women did not have the same rights as men. Women had to give their money to their husbands. They had to pay taxes, but they could not vote. Women felt like American colonists did before the American Revolution. Do you remember their saying, "no taxation without representation"? Mary Ann thought that if she paid taxes she should be able to vote.

Year after year Mary Ann went to Dover to talk to lawmakers. She wanted better laws to help women. She wanted women to get the right to vote. She was ahead of her time. Women did not get the right to vote until after she died, as you will learn in the next chapter.

Sarah Webb Pyle · 1869–1959

Sarah Pyle was born in Wilmington. She helped immigrants in New York City. Then she wanted to help immigrant families in her own hometown. She started a settlement house in Wilmington. She began the Peoples Settlement House in a three-room shack. The house kept growing. It had to move to a much larger building. Soon it had a kindergarten, clubs for children, and classes in cooking, art, and singing.

Sarah Pyle led the People's Settlement House for 50 years and won many awards for her work. Today, a school in Wilmington is named for her.

Help for Immigrants

Life was very hard for all factory workers. It was even harder for those who were immigrants. Many could speak little or no English. They did not know American *customs,* or ways of doing things.

In some of America's big cities there were people who wanted to help the immigrants. One of those people was Jane Addams. She opened a house in Chicago, Illinois, called Hull House. Hull House was also called a settlement house because it helped immigrants settle into their new country. Workers at Hull House helped immigrants learn English. Immigrants could take cooking lessons to learn how to cook like Americans. Immigrants could also see a doctor or a nurse. There were playgrounds for children.

Several settlement houses in Delaware also helped immigrants. The Peoples Settlement House opened in Wilmington. The West End Reading Room also helped people. Each house had kindergartens and sports programs for children. They also had classes for adults and children. Both of these places still help people today.

Immigrant children learned to read and write English at school.

Discrimination and Jim Crow Laws

Discrimination is treating people unfairly just because they are different. Immigrants faced discrimination. African Americans faced even more.

After the Civil War, Delaware and other states made laws called Jim Crow laws. The laws said that black people could not use the same bathrooms or public water fountains as white people. Black people had to sit in separate train cars and in the back seats of trolley cars. They could not eat in the same restaurants or go to the same theaters as white people. Black children and white children could not go to the same schools. Black people got the hardest jobs for the lowest pay if they could find a job at all.

Separating people in school, restaurants, theaters, on buses, and at work because of skin color is called *segregation*. The laws were very unfair. Some white people thought segregation was wrong, but they were too few to be of much help.

Linking the Past to the Present

Do you think people today are judged on just how they look? Do you think this is fair? How does this discrimination cause problems for people?

An old cartoon shows a pilot and a wealthy white man and his wife. They are towing African Americans back to the "Sunny South." Why would the white man and woman want to do this?

3 MEMORY MASTER

1. Describe what it was like to work in a factory.
2. List two reasons why workers went on strike.
3. Who was Sarah Webb Pyle, and what did she do?
4. How did Jim Crow laws hurt African Americans?

PEOPLE TO KNOW

Alexander Graham Bell
Thomas Edison
Bessie Jones

PLACES TO LOCATE

Dover
Seaford
Wilmington

WORDS TO UNDERSTAND

communicate

Inventions Make Life Easier

Many things we use today did not exist years ago. When we flip a light switch, pick up a telephone, or ride in an elevator, we never think about what life was like before these inventions.

Electricity

Over 100 years ago, if you wanted to cook food or heat your house, you had to fill a stove with wood or coal and then light a fire. Today, you only have to turn a knob to get heat.

To get light, you filled a lamp with oil and trimmed the wick once a day. Today, you flip a switch and the lights come on.

Electric power was one of the great inventions of the late 1800s. It changed the way people worked, played, and lived.

Laying the Electrical Tubes

Workers lay long tubes of electric wires. Then they will cover them with dirt. The wires will bring electricity into homes and other buildings. Can you find the horses pulling wagons of supplies?

Thomas Edison invented the first light bulb and created the first electric power station in America. Machines made electricity in power stations. Then the electricity ran through wires to houses, offices, and stores. Soon people used electric lights, washing machines, irons, stoves, refrigerators, and vacuum cleaners.

Wilmington had the first electric system in Delaware. Imagine the excitement of having electric lights in your house for the first time! With just one finger you could turn night into day.

Elevators were run by electricity. After they were invented to take people up and down, people started building taller buildings. Wilmington's first tall building with an elevator had six floors.

Electricity was amazing, but it cost a lot of money to set up an electric system. It was first used in large cities where people lived closer together. Families in small towns and farms did not get electricity for many years.

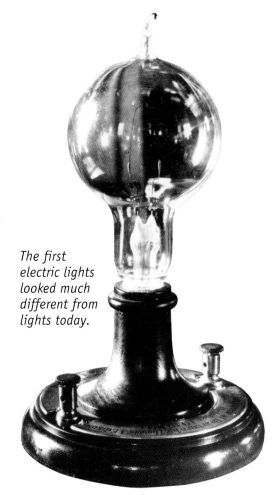

The first electric lights looked much different from lights today.

The Telephone

Alexander Graham Bell's invention made it faster and easier for people to **communicate.** They could talk back and forth on the telephone. At first only businesses and rich people had their own telephones. Many people went to a neighborhood store to use a pay telephone. Later, more families got telephones at home.

An Electric Christmas Display

Bessie Jones was a little girl who lived in Wilmington in 1900. At Christmas, Bessie's neighbor built a tiny village in his house. Electric lights lit up inside the little houses. A tiny man chopped wood. A merry-go-round and a windmill turned all by themselves. Everybody in the neighborhood came to see the display. No one had ever seen anything like it before.

How did people use this early pay telephone?

New Ways to Get Around

Wilmington was Delaware's big city. It kept on growing. Soon it was no longer easy to walk from one end of town to another. A streetcar line was built through the center of the main streets. A streetcar was kind of like a bus. Sometimes the streetcars were called trolley cars, or trolleys. People got on and off at each street corner.

After a while, trolley tracks were built to the factories. They took people to work. People could also ride the trolleys to amusement parks just outside the city. The parks had picnic grounds, rides, stage shows, and dancing.

The streetcars ran on tracks. At first, horses pulled the cars along the tracks. Then trolleys got their power from electricity. This decorated trolley was on its way to the Brandywine Springs Park.

Automobiles

The first automobiles were built in the late 1880s. At first, only rich people could afford to buy them. Doctors bought cars so that they could visit their patients.

Early cars were not easy to start. You had to stand outside the car and turn a crank that was attached to the motor. Once the engine started, you had to jump in fast.

Most streets and roads in Delaware were dirt roads. If the weather was bad, the roads got muddy. Cars often got stuck on the muddy roads.

The man in this photo had to crank his car to get it started. How do we start cars today?

The Delaware Adventure

Sports and Fun for Everyone

People worked hard, but they still had time for fun. There were parades with bands and dances. The circus and traveling shows came to town. Churches had picnics and suppers. People might go to amusement parks or to the beach. Mostly, however, children played at home.

Baseball and Football

Baseball became popular after the Civil War. Children and adults played baseball. Whole towns came out to cheer for their teams.

Football was another popular sport. Clubs, businesses, and colleges had teams. Big crowds came to watch the football games.

Bicycles

Men, women, and children rode bicycles. Most people rode for fun, but there were also bicycle races for prize money.

One of our state's best bicycle riders rode from Wilmington to Dover to see his girlfriend. He went over 100 miles on each trip. The next time you are going a long way away in a car, ask your parents to show you how far 100 miles is. Could you ride a bicycle that far?

The first bicycles had large wheels. Then they were changed to look more like bicycles today.

④ MEMORY MASTER

1. Name three ways people used electricity.
2. What were some of the ways people traveled?

From There to Here

    After the Civil War, Delaware's population grew. The people worked at jobs to make money. Factories in Wilmington got bigger and bigger. Many of the workers were new immigrants from other countries.

    Farmers also needed workers to help plant and harvest fruits and vegetables. Whole families, including little children, worked in the fields and canneries.

    Life for most people was hard. They worked long hours for low pay. Then new laws were passed to protect workers, including women and children. People hoped that life might get a little easier.

    Even though people worked all day, sometimes they were able to play baseball, ride bicycles, and go on picnics. New inventions like electricity and the automobile changed life for everyone.

What Do You Remember?

1. Describe the journey an immigrant had to make from Europe to Delaware.
2. What were Delaware's major industries during this time?
3. What were Delaware's major crops during this time?
4. What were some of the problems of factory workers?
5. Give examples of the kind of work children did.
6. Choose one of the inventions described in Lesson 4 and tell how it changed people's lives.

Activity

Design a Can Label

    Pretend that you own a cannery. You want to get people to buy your product. Draw or paint a label that shows one of the fruits or vegetables you want to sell in the cans.

Activity

Population, 1870–1910

This bar graph shows the number of people who lived in Delaware during different years. Use the graph to compare information.

Year	Population
1870	125,000
1880	147,000
1890	168,000
1900	185,000
1910	202,000

1. Did the number of people rise or fall from 1870 to 1910?
2. How many more people lived in Delaware in 1910 than in 1870?
3. Which year began a new century? (100 years)
4. How many years does the graph cover?

Activity

The World in Your Closet

You read in this chapter how people in Delaware manufactured railroad and subway cars that were shipped to many countries of the world. You read how people in our state canned fruit and vegetables and shipped them to faraway places.

People in Delaware still make things that are used all over the world. People in Delaware also buy things that are made in other countries. Look around your house to see if you can find items that were made in other places. Read the labels on your clothes. Where was your food grown? Was your family car made in another country?

Write down the item and where it was made or grown. Then find the places on a map. How many countries and states did you find?

Item	Country or State Where It Was Made
• blue shirt	• India
• bananas	• Mexico

Delaware in Modern Times

"*Our newest immigrants come from all around the globe. Some have come from countries in Asia. Many other immigrants come from Spanish-speaking countries. These people are seeking jobs and a better life for themselves and their children.*"

—*Barbara Benson, 2005*

Timeline of Events

1914–1918
World War I

1917
The United States enters World War I.

1919
Pierre du Pont starts to build new schools.

1920
The 19th Amendment to the U.S. Constitution gives women the right to vote.

1923
Cecile Steele begins a chicken industry in Sussex County.

1924
The DuPont Highway is completed.

1929
The Great Depression begins.

1939
The world's first nylon plant opens in Seaford.

1941
The United States enters the war.

1939–1945
World War II

1910

1920

1930

1940

The city of Wilmington has been changing for over 350 years. Today you can see a mixture of buildings from differents times in its history. All of Delaware's cities have their own unique story. What can you learn about the city nearest your home?

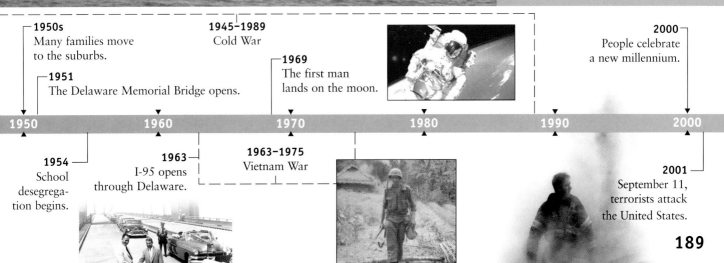

1950s
Many families move to the suburbs.

1945–1989
Cold War

2000
People celebrate a new millennium.

1951
The Delaware Memorial Bridge opens.

1969
The first man lands on the moon.

1950   1960   1970   1980   1990   2000

1954
School desegregation begins.

1963
I-95 opens through Delaware.

1963–1975
Vietnam War

2001
September 11, terrorists attack the United States.

PEOPLE TO KNOW

Wallace Carothers
Henry Ford
Pierre S. du Pont
T. Coleman du Pont
Franklin D. Roosevelt
Cecile Steele

PLACES TO LOCATE

Bethany Beach
Dover
Georgetown
Newark
Ocean View
Rehoboth Beach
Seaford
Selbyville
Wilmington

WORDS TO UNDERSTAND

allies
depression
paved
submarine

A Train Ride in 1900

If you had a time machine that could take you back to the year 1900, you would find life in Delaware very different from life today. Pretend you lived back then. It is a hot summer, and you and your family are going to Rehoboth Beach for a vacation. How will you get there? What will you see along the way? What will you wear?

Your family decides to travel by train. Your father checks the schedule to see when the train will leave the Wilmington station. You pack your bag. Your family jumps on a trolley and rides to the train station. All of you find a seat on the train. It sends up puffs of black dust as it leaves the station. The train stops at every town to pick up new passengers and let others off.

"All aboard the Rehoboth Boardwalk Train!" In 1910, People usually rode to the train station in a carriage pulled by horses.

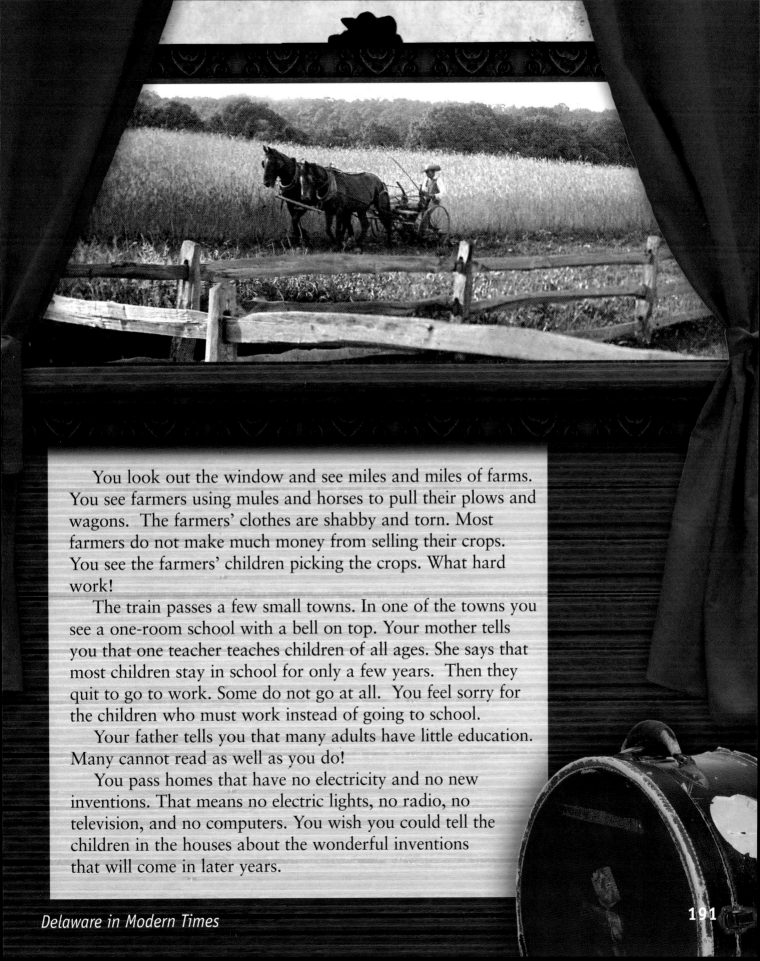

You look out the window and see miles and miles of farms. You see farmers using mules and horses to pull their plows and wagons. The farmers' clothes are shabby and torn. Most farmers do not make much money from selling their crops. You see the farmers' children picking the crops. What hard work!

The train passes a few small towns. In one of the towns you see a one-room school with a bell on top. Your mother tells you that one teacher teaches children of all ages. She says that most children stay in school for only a few years. Then they quit to go to work. Some do not go at all. You feel sorry for the children who must work instead of going to school.

Your father tells you that many adults have little education. Many cannot read as well as you do!

You pass homes that have no electricity and no new inventions. That means no electric lights, no radio, no television, and no computers. You wish you could tell the children in the houses about the wonderful inventions that will come in later years.

Rehoboth Beach was a different place in the early 1900s. What kinds of swimsuits are the people wearing? What are the people doing? What other clues tell you this photograph was taken a long time ago?

At the Beach

Finally, the train enters the town's main street. The train station is located about two blocks from the boardwalk. You see people on the boardwalk dressed in their best clothes. The women wear long dresses and fancy hats with flowers and feathers on them. The men wear suits and ties. They also wear hats. Families playing on the beach and swimming in the ocean are wearing heavy woolen bathing suits that go down to their knees!

You notice something on your trip that puzzles you. Black people and white people are hardly ever together in the same place. Your parents tell you that laws of the time say that black people and white people have to ride on separate cars on the train. The only black people who are permitted on the beach are servants who take care of white children. You feel sad that all the children can't enjoy the ocean waves together.

The train stops, and your family picks up their bags. You have learned a lot, but your long ride is over. You are ready to splash in the ocean!

The Delaware Adventure

Here Come Cars and Trucks

In the early years of the 20th century, gasoline-powered automobiles were a new invention. Only a few rich people could afford a car. The roads were so bad that cars often got stuck in the mud.

T. Coleman du Pont was president of the DuPont Company. He loved cars. In college he had studied about how to build good roads and bridges. He thought automobiles and trucks could lead to a brighter future for everyone. But first, the state needed *paved* roads.

Du Pont decided to build a highway the length of Delaware. The highway was built through swamps, forests, and farms. It began near Selbyville. Then it passed by Georgetown and Dover as it moved toward Wilmington. The DuPont Highway was the first modern paved road in Delaware.

Thick mud was an enemy to drivers. Still, cars were far better than horses and wagons.

T. Coleman du Pont loved the new cars. He paid to have a modern highway built through Delaware.

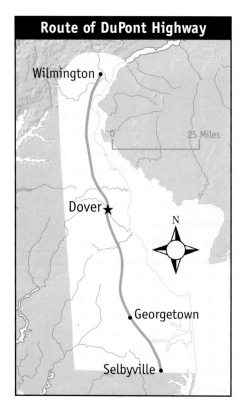

Route of DuPont Highway

Wilmington

0   25 Miles

Dover ★

N

Georgetown

Selbyville

By the time the new highway was finished, an automobile maker in Michigan named Henry Ford had found a way to make cars and trucks quickly and cheaply. Then more families could afford a car. Farmers and businesses could buy trucks.

The DuPont Highway and the invention of trucks changed farming in Delaware. Farmers could drive their crops to stores in the city instead of paying the railroads to take the fruits, vegetables, grain, and meat. Farmers could harvest fruit one day and have it in a store or restaurant the next morning.

Activity

Connecting Cities Today

Part of the old DuPont Highway is now called Route 113. Another part is called Route 13. Find these highways on a road map. What cities do they connect?

Cecile Steele and the Chicken Industry

Cecile Steele and her family lived on a farm near the village of Ocean View. Like many farm wives, Mrs. Steele kept a few chickens. She sold their eggs for extra money. Then one year she had a lot more baby chickens than she needed.

Mrs. Steele raised the chicks until they were large enough to eat. Then she packed them in a truck and sent them up the DuPont Highway to city stores. She got a good price for her chickens. Word spread about what she had done. She had found a new way for farmers to make money.

Soon raising chickens became a big business in Sussex County. Farmers also made money raising soybeans and corn for the chickens to eat.

Processing plants were built. Large trucks carried the chickens to cities. From there, they went to grocery stores and restaurants.

Soldiers wave to their families as they ride off to war.

I WANT YOU
FOR U.S. ARMY
NEAREST RECRUITING STATION

Posters like this tried to get men to leave their homes and sign up to be soldiers. The man in the tall hat is "Uncle Sam." Who did he represent?

World War I

World War I started in Europe when Germany attacked France. England and Russia declared war on Germany. Americans wanted to help England and France fight the war. The DuPont Company sold explosives and gunpowder to England and France. Supplies were sent across the Atlantic Ocean in ships. Then German *submarines* sank some of the ships.

Leaders in the United States said the Germans had no right to sink American ships. The United States entered the war against Germany. It was a terrible war. Millions of people were killed. Cities in Europe were bombed. Finally, England and her *allies* won the war. In war, an ally is a friendly country that fights on your side.

Reforming Education

The men from the United States who joined the army in World War I were tested to see if they were fit to be soldiers. The tests showed that many men in Delaware were not very healthy. Many also could not read or write or do much math. Leaders in the state were worried. What could they do to solve those problems?

People thought the state needed better schools. The old one-room schools could not do the job. Pierre du Pont wanted to help improve Delaware's schools. The DuPont Company had made a lot of money selling gunpowder during World War I. Pierre du Pont spent some of the money he earned to build modern school buildings in Delaware towns.

Pierre S. du Pont spent millions of dollars to make better schools.

New School Buildings

Imagine how exciting it was for the children when they first entered their new schools. The schools had large windows to let the sun into the rooms. Many had gyms and lunchrooms. The one-room schools had only dirty outhouses behind the school, but the new schools had indoor toilets, sinks, and water fountains.

A College for Teachers

It was important to have well-trained teachers to teach in the new schools. Women's clubs and a farmers' group asked the state government to help. Government leaders agreed to start a women's college in Newark. The college taught young women to be teachers. The college also prepared them to go into jobs in science and other fields. The college later became part of the University of Delaware.

The Bear White School was built in 1865. How were the modern schools better than this school?

The Delaware Adventure

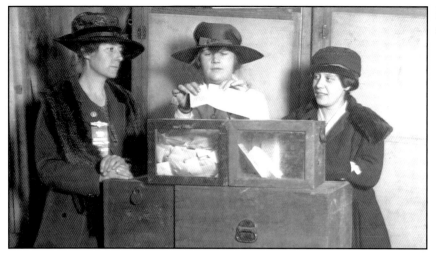

Women were proud to cast their first votes.

VOTES FOR WOMEN

For the work of a day.
For the taxes we pay.
For the Laws we obey.
We want something to say.

Women Win the Right to Vote

Everywhere in the country, women were demanding the right to be equal to men. Women wanted a better education. Women who worked wanted to be paid more money. Most of all, women wanted the right to vote. It did not seem fair that the law kept half of the people from voting.

Women all over the United States gave speeches and marched in parades. Their efforts finally paid off. Congress passed the Nineteenth Amendment to the U.S. Constitution to give women the right to vote. Then the amendment had to be ratified, or approved, by 36 states.

An Important Vote

Soon 35 states had ratified. Only one more state was needed. All eyes turned to Delaware. Women from other states came to Dover and gave speeches. They paraded around, carrying signs. But the Delaware leaders refused to ratify. The women were very angry. They left Dover and went to Tennessee. The vote there was very close. By one vote, Tennessee leaders voted to ratify! The amendment was finally added to the U.S. Constitution. Women in every state got the right to vote.

Taking Sides

Florence Bayard Hilles was the sister, daughter, granddaughter, and great-granddaughter of United States senators. She thought it was unfair that she had to pay taxes but could not vote. She gave speeches in Delaware and held signs at the White House in Washington, D.C. The police there put her in jail for causing trouble.

Another woman, Mary Wilson Thompson, disagreed. She thought women could do good things without voting. She thought men were better at government. She worked very hard to keep Delaware's leaders from ratifying the new amendment.

Nylon

······· **Activity** ·······

Nylon—A Miracle Fiber

Nylon is not just used for clothes. Learn more about nylon. Research on the Internet, in encyclopedias, and books. How many uses for nylon did you find? Can you find any nylon in your home?

Do you remember what people wore to go swimming 100 years ago? They wore swimming suits made from wool. The suits were heavy and itchy. Today, you wear a suit made from soft fabric that was developed by scientists. The fabrics were invented in Delaware.

Wallace Carothers, a scientist at the DuPont Company, invented nylon. Nylon was the first man-made fiber, or thread. The thread was woven into cloth for clothes. The DuPont Company built its first nylon factory at Seaford. Many people got jobs at the factory. Nylon became very popular because it was strong, but light. It did not wrinkle. It kept its shape. Women especially liked nylon stockings.

After the success of nylon, DuPont scientists invented other fibers. Today, many of our clothes are made from them, including our swimming suits.

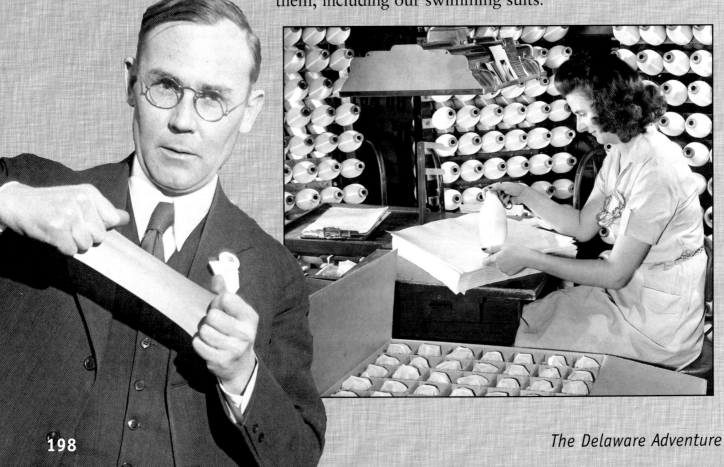

Wallace Carothers' invention changed everything. The woman is inspecting spools of nylon thread.

The Great Depression

A *depression* is a time when many people can't make enough money to take care of their families. They want to work, but they can't find jobs.

The depression of the 1930s was the worst depression the United States has ever known. It is called the Great Depression.

Farmers in Delaware felt the depression first. Food prices went down, so farmers earned less money. Many factory workers lost their jobs. They had to survive as best they could. They planted vegetable gardens for food. They mended old clothes over and over.

People tried to help each other. People with jobs gave up some of their pay to help those who had no jobs. Many groups and churches pitched in. But life was hard during the Great Depression.

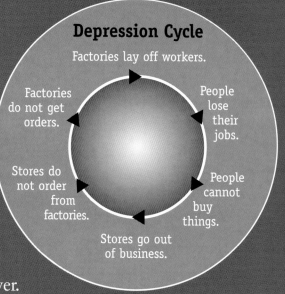

Depression Cycle

Factories lay off workers.

People lose their jobs.

People cannot buy things.

Stores go out of business.

Stores do not order from factories.

Factories do not get orders.

The New Deal

President Franklin D. Roosevelt had a plan. He called his plan the New Deal. The government loaned farmers money so they could stay in business. Young people were trained for jobs. Children got free school lunches. The president started projects to make jobs. In Delaware, the government paid workers to drain swamps to get rid of mosquitoes. Workers built or fixed highways, schools, public buildings, and bridges.

Men were paid to drain ditches.

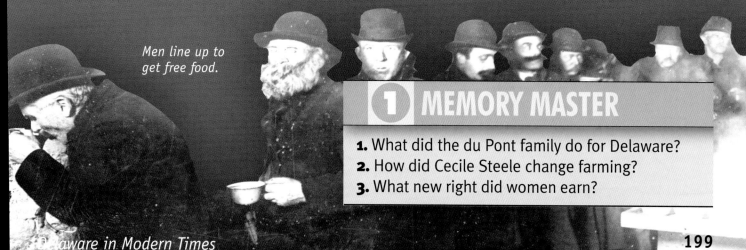

Men line up to get free food.

1 MEMORY MASTER

1. What did the du Pont family do for Delaware?
2. How did Cecile Steele change farming?
3. What new right did women earn?

PEOPLE TO KNOW

James Connor
John F. Kennedy
Littleton Mitchell
George Welch

PLACES TO LOCATE

Germany
Japan
Russia (the Soviet Union)
Pearl Harbor, Hawaii
Frederica
Milford
Cape Henlopen

WORDS TO UNDERSTAND

astronaut
dictator
parachute
satellite

U.S. sailors sprayed water at the flames of burning ships after the bombing of Pearl Harbor.

Attack on Pearl Harbor

December 7, 1941, was a terrible day in history. Japanese airplanes dropped bombs on U.S. ships at Pearl Harbor, Hawaii. Several large ships were sunk. Many sailors died. The attack on Pearl Harbor was a surprise. It brought the United States into World War II.

George S. Welch, Delaware's Pearl Harbor Hero

George Welch was an Army Air Force pilot from Wilmington. He was near Pearl Harbor when the attack began. He raced to an airfield, climbed into a plane, and took off. Then he fearlessly attacked a group of 12 Japanese planes and shot down two of them. Later, he shot down two other Japanese planes. Welch won an award for his "coolness under fire against overwhelming odds." President Franklin Roosevelt invited him to the White House. New York City gave him a big parade. Then he returned to the war.

Children collected old beds, pots, bicycles, or anything made of metal. The metal was made into parts of tanks, planes, guns, and other things the soldiers needed to fight the war.

Life in Delaware During World War II

World War II was fought in Europe and in Asia. It was also fought in the Atlantic and Pacific Oceans. Over 30,000 men and women from Delaware fought in battles on land and sea around the world.

The war changed the lives of everyone in Delaware. There had been few jobs during the Great Depression. After the war started, there were many jobs in factories. Factories along the Christina River built hundreds of ships, boats, and landing craft. In southern Delaware farmers raised food to feed the soldiers and sailors. There was even a movie made about Delaware's chicken farms. It was called "Your Chicken Goes to War."

Everyone at home wanted to help win the war. People planted gardens called "victory gardens" to grow food. This meant that more food could be sent to soldiers overseas.

People took turns looking at the sky for enemy planes that might attack. Airplane spotters took turns at 69 towers across our state. Someone was on the lookout day and night, every day of the week. Luckily, the enemy never attacked the mainland of the United States.

Making Things Last

One way to be sure that our soldiers had everything they needed was to limit what people at home could buy. People could only buy a small amount of sugar, meat, butter, coffee, gas, tires, and other things.

Each family was given ration stamps to buy these items every month. When the stamps ran out, the family had to wait until the next month to buy more.

The "C" stamps were for gasoline. The others were for food and other items. Farmers grew extra grain and vegetables and raised hogs and chickens. They sent the extra food to the troops.

I'm Proud... my husband *wants* me to do my part

SEE YOUR U. S. EMPLOYMENT SERVICE
WAR MANPOWER COMMISSION

Women at Work

During the war the government needed nylon to make *parachutes* for airplane pilots. The parachutes would help soldiers who had to get to the ground if a plane was hit in the sky. The only way to meet the demand was to hire women. The women were very good workers. Women also helped build ships and make weapons for soldiers.

Delaware's Defenses

Our state played important roles in the defense of the state and the nation. New Castle Army Air Base near Wilmington had the first training center for female pilots. These women flew planes from one place to another in America. Sometimes they flew planes from a factory to an airbase, or from one base to another.

Planes from Dover Air Force Base watched the skies over the Delaware Bay. Fighter pilots trained at the base. The most exciting activity was top secret. Scientists tested rockets there. Rockets were a new invention.

Fort Miles was on the sand dunes of Cape Henlopen. The fort was built to guard the coast and protect ships from German submarines. Fort Miles did not look like forts of the past. It had no high stone walls. In fact, the fort could not be seen from the ocean or the bay. Large guns that could sink a submarine were hidden behind the sand dunes. People stood on towers to spot enemy submarines. You can still see the towers along the Delaware coast.

Women pilots called WASPs wore uniforms like these.

Littleton Mitchell and the Tuskegee Airmen

Soldiers were segregated in World War II. A program was created at Tuskegee, Alabama, to train black pilots. They were called the Tuskegee Airmen. They proved to be among the very best pilots in the U.S. Air Force.

Littleton Mitchell, from Milford, was one of the trainers. His mother had told him, "You are as good as anyone else." He inspired his men. He later became a civil rights leader in Delaware.

The Delaware Adventure

People celebrated in the streets when they learned the war was over.

James P. Connor

James P. Connor fought the Germans in Europe. He was shot three times, but he kept on fighting.

When his commanding officer was killed, Connor took command of the nine men in his unit who were still alive. He told the men, "They can hit me, but they can't stop me." Connor won the highest medal for his bravery in the war.

Victory!

It took years of hard fighting and the deaths of millions of people before the United States and its allies won the war with Germany. Then the United States still had to win the war with Japan. To do that, the United States used a new secret weapon called the atomic bomb. American pilots dropped bombs on two Japanese cities. The powerful bombs killed and wounded thousands of people in the cities, but the bombing ended the war. No more people would have to die.

The Cold War Begins

When peace came, it was not as peaceful as people had hoped. At the time, Russia was part of the Soviet Union. The Soviet Union and the United States had different kinds of governments. Both countries feared attack by the other. For many years there was a Cold War between the two countries. It was called that because neither side ever attacked the other.

Each country built a large army, navy, and air force. Both also did secret research to build stronger and faster weapons. Each side wanted weapons so powerful that the other would be afraid to attack. It took a long, long time, but the Cold War ended without a shot being fired.

Linking the Past to the Present

Today, Dover Air Force Base is home to the world's largest cargo planes. Each plane is almost as long as a football field and as tall as a six-story building. You can put four buses on one plane. The cargo planes fly all over the world.

Delaware in Modern Times

Delaware in the Space Race

The United States and the Soviet Union each wanted to be first to explore space. The Soviets were the first to put a satellite called *Sputnik* into space. The satellite circled the earth and sent back information.

President John F. Kennedy said that the United States could do something even better. He called on the United States to put a man on the moon.

A company in Delaware agreed to make space suits for the *astronauts.* Astronauts are people who go into space on rocket ships. The suits that astronauts wear are very hard to make. If everything is not perfect, the astronaut might die.

Women worked together at a factory in Frederica. They sewed the astronauts' suits and gloves. The astronauts who landed on the moon wore suits made in Delaware. The suits worked perfectly.

The Delaware Adventure

Wars in Asia

The United States and other countries fought in other wars. Soldiers from the United States were sent to help South Korea. South Korea was being taken over by North Korea.

The Vietnam War began as a war between North and South Vietnam. The war was the longest war in the history of the United States. It lasted over 10 years. Thousands of American soldiers lost their lives in Vietnam. Some Americans saw the war as a fight for freedom. Other Americans believed we had no business in Vietnam.

When the war finally ended, many Vietnamese and other Asian people did not feel safe in their country. Many made a long, hard journey to the United States. Today, their children and grandchildren are Americans.

Linking the Past to the Present

Ask your family if your relatives fought in Vietnam. Does your family have anyone fighting in war today? Where are they fighting? What kind of work are they doing there?

Vietnam was a hot, humid jungle. The people there were mostly farmers.

2 MEMORY MASTER

1. What event brought the United States into World War II?
2. How did the people of our state help during the war?
3. What was the Space Race?
4. How did some Delaware women help astronauts who walked on the moon?

PEOPLE TO KNOW

George W. Bush
Dr. Martin Luther King Jr.
Louis Redding

PLACES TO LOCATE

Asia
Central America
China
India
Japan
Mexico
Pakistan
Puerto Rico
South Korea

WORDS TO UNDERSTAND

Hispanic
integration
terrorism

What does the sign in front of the house say to convince buyers to move in?

Cars and Suburbs

Life changed a lot after more and more people got automobiles. They no longer had to depend on trolleys and buses to get to work. They could drive their cars to the new office buildings and factories that were built beyond the towns and cities. A factory that assembled automobiles was built at Newark. Another was built west of Wilmington. Food processing and clothing factories were built in Dover.

Once families had cars, they no longer had to live in cities near their jobs. Many families moved to new communities outside of town. The new homes were built on land that had once been farms. These communities next to cities were called suburbs.

The suburbs changed the way people shopped. Before, people took a trolley or a horse and wagon and shopped in many different kinds of stores in the cities. Then a lot of families got cars. Where would they park while they shopped? There were few parking lots.

Business owners got an idea. Why not build shopping centers and shopping malls in the suburbs? The malls could be closer to where many people lived, and they could be surrounded with large parking lots. People who lived in the suburbs loved the idea. People who owned the stores in the cities, however, were not happy. Stores in every city lost business.

New Highways and Bridges

More cars meant that people needed more highways and bridges. The Delaware Memorial Bridge was built across the Delaware River. The bridge is a memorial to the soldiers and sailors who died in World War II. Traffic was so great a second bridge was added.

A large highway called I-95 was built all along the coast. The "I" stands for "interstate." Interstates go through many states. Since there are no traffic lights on these large roads, they make driving faster.

Traffic also got so great on the DuPont Highway that Route 1 was built between Wilmington and Dover. Route 1 has a big bridge to take traffic over the Chesapeake and Delaware Canal.

What do you think?

Why is it important for a community to have good roads?

On the day the Memorial Bridge opened in 1951, the governors of New Jersey and Delaware shook hands.

More than 80,000 vehicles cross the Delaware Memorial Bridge every day.

A realtor is a person who sells houses. This Civil Rights march was protesting unfair discrimination. At the time, blacks were not allowed to buy homes in many neighborhoods where only white people lived.

The Struggle for Civil Rights

African Americans served their country well during World War II. They fought as Tuskegee Airmen and in the army and the navy. They worked in factories that made guns and tanks. Like all Americans, blacks were fighting to keep America free. But the country was not free for them. Segregation kept blacks from the best schools, the best neighborhoods, and the best jobs.

After the war, African Americans demanded more rights. Their actions began the Civil Rights Movement. They wanted to end segregation. Instead, the people wanted *integration.* They wanted people of all races to go to school together. They wanted people of all races to be able to work in the same office or buy houses in any neighborhood. They wanted all children to play on the same beach and in the same parks.

Dr. Martin Luther King Jr.

Young black leaders worked hard to end segregation. One leader was Dr. Martin Luther King Jr. He was a minister in Georgia. He led peaceful marches and protests. He reminded everyone that our nation was founded on the belief that "all men are created equal."

Both black people and white people joined Dr. King's marches. Thousands of men and women took part in a march in Washington, D.C. That is where Dr. King gave his famous "I Have a Dream" speech. Sadly, a few years later, Dr. King was murdered. Americans were shocked and sad.

Integrating Delaware's Schools

It took a long time for all the states to obey the new civil rights laws. Delaware's public schools were still segregated. Black children and white children went to different schools. There were very few high schools for black students.

A civil rights group in Delaware went to court to ask that children of all races be allowed to go to school together. The group's lawyer was Louis Redding. Mr. Redding said that the schools for black children were not as good as the schools for white children.

In court, a Delaware judge agreed with Louis Redding. But the United States Supreme Court had the final power to decide if schools could remain segregated. The Supreme Court made the Delaware case a part of a group of cases from other states. In a famous case called *Brown v. Board of Education*, the Supreme Court said that segregation was wrong. After that ruling the schools in Delaware were integrated. Black and white children started to sit together in the same classrooms.

Linking the Past to the Present

Today, all forms of segregation in public places are against the law.

Delaware PORTRAIT

Louis Redding • 1901–1999

Louis Redding grew up in Wilmington. He came from a very smart family. His brother became a college professor and his sisters became teachers. Louis went to college and became a lawyer. He was the first black lawyer in Delaware. He was the only black lawyer in the state for 25 years.

Redding fought for new laws that would give equal rights to African Americans. His most famous work was to end segregation in public schools.

Today, a statue of Redding and two young students stands outside the entrance to the city/county building in Wilmington that is named for Redding.

The Pentagon

A New Kind of War— September 11, 2001

On the morning of September 11, 2001, something happened that changed our country. Americans watched in disbelief as they learned that terrorists had taken control of four airplanes. The terrorists flew two of them into the World Trade Center Towers in New York City. Another plane flew into the Pentagon in Washington, D.C. People also learned that another plane crashed into a field in Pennsylvania.

Over 3,000 people died in the attacks. Nearly 350 firefighters died trying to save the lives of people trapped in the explosion of the Towers. The first war of the 21st century in America began when President George W. Bush declared a war on *terrorism.* It was a new kind of war.

Some Delawareans were in the World Trade Towers when the planes hit them. Others from Delaware witnessed the scene in horror and disbelief from their seats on a train coming into New York City.

People from our state gathered together to express their anger and sorrow. Students at the University of Delaware lit candles for each person who died in the plane crashes in New York, Pennsylvania, and Washington. People in Delaware and all over the country put American flags on their houses and lawns.

Americans raised millions of dollars to help the families who had lost loved ones in the terrorist attacks. The government increased security all over America. It sent soldiers to the Middle East and other places to fight terrorism.

America was targeted for attack because we're the brightest beacon for freedom and opportunity in the world. And no one will keep that light from shining.

—President George W. Bush

The Delaware Adventure

Delaware in the 21st Century

Delaware has changed in the last 100 years. In 1900, only 185,000 people lived in our state. By the year 2000, almost 784,000 people lived here.

New Delawareans

In recent times, new immigrants have come to live in Delaware. They come from all around the globe. Some people have come from countries in Asia. China, South Korea, Japan, India, and Pakistan are some of these countries.

Many immigrants have come from Spanish-speaking countries. The people are sometimes called *Hispanics* because they speak Spanish. Hispanics have come to Delaware from Puerto Rico, Mexico, and other countries in Central America. They are seeking jobs and a better life for themselves and their children.

A Trip Through Delaware Today

Other things in our state have also changed a lot. Remember our imaginary train trip from Wilmington to Rehoboth Beach 100 years ago? If you make that trip today, you will ride in a car or a bus. You will see many more houses and fewer farms. The suburbs have moved out from the cities and towns.

South of Dover you will see the massive Dover Air Force Base. Then look for the long, low chicken houses on the farms. As you get near the beaches, you will see many vacation houses, outlet malls, and restaurants along the road. At the beach you will see people of every race walking, sitting, and swimming.

Yes, Delaware has changed a lot in the last 100 years. It will keep changing in your lifetime.

Compare the clothes of the men and women at the beach. Things have really changed in 100 years!

3 MEMORY MASTER

1. Choose one topic from this lesson and read it again. What did you learn the second time that you didn't remember the first time?

From There to Here

Delaware has changed a lot in the past 100 years. The state built modern highways and two bridges across the Delaware River. Women got the vote and got better jobs. Farmers began raising chickens and the grains to feed them. Nylon became an important state product. Modern schools replaced one-room schools. The public schools were integrated. All children could learn together.

Delaware was also part of larger changes in the world. The United States fought two world wars, a Cold War with the Soviet Union, and wars in Asia. Men landed on the moon.

People from all over the world have moved to Delaware. Most of the immigrants today are Asians or Hispanics. Everyone works together to make our state a great place to live.

Technology Tie-In

What holds up a suspension bridge? Research the Delaware Memorial Bridge and the Chesapeake and Delaware Canal Bridge. What holds up the roads?

Activity

Role Play

Some of the events in this chapter would be fun to act out. Choose one of these events. Then work with a group to act out the event. Decide who will act out different parts. Choose names for the people. Decide what each person will say and what actions they will use. If you can, make a video of your skit.

- Cars and Trucks Help the Farming Industry
- Cecile Steele and the Chicken Industry
- Women Win the Right to Vote
- Delaware's Defenses During World War II
- Delaware in the Space Race

Geography 🌍 Tie-In

I-95 goes through northern Delaware. It is part of an interestate highway system. Where does I-95 begin in the South, and where does it end in the North?

Activity

What If?

Talk with your class about each of these subjects. For each one, make a list on the board of ways your life would be different if history had turned out differently.

1. What if your family did not have a car or a truck? How would your life be different? Where would you live? How would you shop? How would you get to sports events? What else would you have to do in a different way?
2. What if your school was a one-room school? Would you have the same teacher? What would you miss? What would you like?
3. What if you were an immigrant to Delaware? What things would be hard for you? What things would you like? What would it be like to go to school if you did not speak English?
4. What if the United States and its allies had lost one of the world wars? How might your life be different?

Activity

Research, Write, and Draw

Use library books and the Internet to find out more about one of these subjects. Write a short paper about it. Draw a picture to go with your report, or make a poster or a model showing what you learned. Explain it to the class.

- World War II
- The Civil Rights Movement
- Astronauts on the Moon
- September 11, 2001 Terrorist Attack

Delaware in Modern Times

Government for the Nation and the State

"*Governments, like clocks, go from the motion men give them.*"

—*William Penn*

Chapter 9

Legislative Hall in Dover is home to our state government. Our state laws are made here. Have you visited this building?

amendment
democracy
document
graffiti
representative

Governments for the World

There are nearly 200 countries in the world. They are all different sizes, from very large to very small. Each country has its own form of government. Some are ruled by a king, with or without a legislature. Others are ruled by an all-powerful leader. Many have a *democracy*. In a democracy, the people rule.

Government for the United States

The United States of America is one of the largest countries in the world. It is also the most powerful nation in the world. That is why it is often called a "superpower."

The United States is a democracy. The people elect *representatives* to make the laws. They also elect the president of the country and other leaders.

Delaware is one of the 50 states that make up the United States of America. Delaware's people are part of our country's democratic government.

Government Is for Us

Did you know that government is part of your daily life? The last time you checked out a book at the library, went to a public school, or played in a city park, you were using a part of government. Here are some of the most important things governments do:

Each country in the world has a flag. Do you know which countries these flags represent?

☑ Provide Services

Our government provides many services. Public schools, parks, roads, and the help of police workers are all government services. You will learn more about services later in this chapter.

☑ Protect Rights

One of the most important things our government does is protect our rights. Let's say you leave your new bike outside. While you are inside playing, someone steals your bike. You are mad because you know this is not fair. That bike was your property! What can you do?

You can go to the police. They will try to find your bike and catch the person who stole it. We have laws against stealing. What if someone tried to hurt you or your family? That is also against the law. It is your right to feel safe.

You also have the right to live in a free country. This means you have the right to belong to the religion of your choice, or to no religion at all. People have the right to gather together in large groups to talk about ideas. The government cannot tell newspapers what to print. Our laws protect these important rights.

☑ Provide Order

What if there were no traffic lights or stop signs, and three cars came to a corner at the same time? If no cars stopped, there would be an accident.

How do we know whose turn it is to go first? We know because we have rules. Rules tell us who has to stop and who gets to go. They make things run smoothly. They also make things safer.

People in a community and in our nation agree to follow certain rules or laws. If someone breaks a law, the person might have to pay a fine or go to jail.

Citizens have the responsibility to obey traffic signs. Laws help keep people safe.

Important Documents

The Declaration of Independence

The government of the United States of America is based on some very important *documents.* They state the beliefs of our people. They also state how our government must be run. These documents put the people of the country at the center of our government.

In an earlier chapter you learned about the Declaration of Independence. It stated the main ideas of American democracy. It said that "all men are created equal." It said that all people have the right to "life, liberty, and the pursuit of happiness." It said that everyone has rights, and that government exists to protect our rights, not to take them away.

Thomas Jefferson wrote the Declaration of Independence. This statue stands in the Jefferson Memorial in Washington, D.C.

The Constitution

You read in an earlier chapter that about four years after the end of the American Revolution, our nation worked to have a stronger government. Men from each state gathered in Philadelphia. They wrote a document called the Constitution of the United States of America. It is the most important document in the United States.

The men who wrote the Constitution did not want a king or a queen to rule the people. For over 200 years the people in our country have voted for representatives and a president who make our laws and lead our country. Here are a few of the Constitution's most important ideas:

- Government by the people
- Three branches of government
- Levels of government—
  federal and state

The first copy of the Constitution was written by hand. Can you read the first three words?

The Delaware Adventure

The Bill of Rights

After the Constitution was written and approved by the states, many people thought something needed to be added. They wanted a clear list of the rights belonging to Americans. They wanted to be sure that the government could never take away these rights.

Ten changes, or *amendments,* were added to the Constitution. They are called the Bill of Rights.

1st Amendment:
Freedom of religion: You can worship as you wish, or not at all. The government cannot choose one religion for the whole country.

Freedom of speech: You can express your opinion about any subject without being arrested. You can even criticize the government. But what you say can't cause danger or harm to others.

Freedom of the press: The government cannot tell people what they can or cannot print in newspapers or books.

Freedom of assembly: You have the right to join and meet with any group. However, you cannot commit crimes with the group.

2nd Amendment:
Right to bear arms: You can own guns for hunting and other legal activities.

3rd Amendment:
Right to not have soldiers in your home during peacetime: In the past, kings had made people feed and house soldiers not only during wars but in times of peace.

4th Amendment:
Freedom from improper search and seizure: You have a right to privacy. But if the police have a reason to think you have something illegal in your home, they can get a search warrant and search your home.

5th, 6th, and 7th Amendments:
These have to do with rights people have if they commit crimes. They include the right to a speedy trial and a trial by a jury.

8th Amendment:
No cruel or unusual punishment is allowed.

9th Amendment:
People have other rights not named in the Bill of Rights.

10th Amendment:
A great deal of power will remain with the states. The people did not want the federal government to have all the power.

What do you think?

Does freedom of speech mean you can put *graffiti* on public property? Can you tell lies that harm others? How can we use our freedoms so they don't hurt anyone else?

Three Branches of Government

The U.S. Constitution gives power to three branches of national government. Each branch has its own powers. Each branch also limits the power of the other two. That way, no single branch can become too powerful.

Look at this giant government tree to see all the important things that go on in each branch.

Executive Branch

The executive branch carries out the laws. The president is the head of the executive branch. Find the people who are talking with the president.

Legislative Branch (Congress)

The men and women who make our laws work in the House and in the Senate. They come to Washington, D.C. from all 50 states. Find the people who are giving speeches. They are talking about the laws they want to be passed.

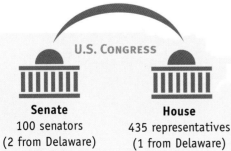

U.S. CONGRESS

Senate
100 senators
(2 from Delaware)

House
435 representatives
(1 from Delaware)

Judicial Branch

The courts make up the judicial branch. Courts decide what the laws mean. They must make sure laws do not go against the Constitution and its Bill of Rights.

A judge listens to cases and rules in a court. A jury is a group of people who also listen to cases and decide if a person has broken a law.

Find the judge, jury, and court reporter. The court reporter writes down everything said in court.

Voting

It is important to remember that in a democracy, the people choose their leaders by voting. If representatives don't make laws the people want, the people might vote for someone else next time. Find the people voting. Then find the leaders climbing up the tree to serve in one of the branches of government.

1 MEMORY MASTER

1. Name the most important document in our country.
2. Name five rights of American citizens.
3. In our country, people vote for _____ to make laws.
4. Name the branches of national government and tell what each branch does.

WORDS TO UNDERSTAND

budget
candidate
county seat
veto
volunteers

Delaware's State Constitution

The 50 states of our country are not all alike. They have different land, people, and industries. Even so, the people in each state have to obey the laws made by the U.S. Congress. They have to follow the U.S. Constitution.

Each state also has its own state government. Each state has its own constitution. The leaders of each state can decide what is best for the people in their state.

Our state's constitution is a lot like the U.S. Constitution. It says all power comes from the people. It includes a Bill of Rights. It includes three branches of government. Each branch has certain jobs.

The Legislative Branch: The General Assembly

Delaware's General Assembly works like the U.S. Congress. It has two parts. They are the Senate and the House of Representatives.

The General Assembly starts meeting each year in January and ends on the last day of June. The men and women meet in Legislative Hall in Dover. You and your family can sit in special seats in the balcony and watch the members of the General Assembly talk about new laws they want to be passed.

Members of the General Assembly do these jobs:
- Make laws for the state.
- Decide what taxes people will pay.
- Work with the governor to set the state's *budget.* A budget tells how much money the government can spend to do its work.

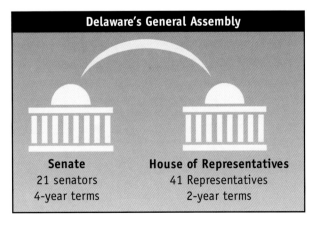

Delaware's General Assembly

Senate
21 senators
4-year terms

House of Representatives
41 Representatives
2-year terms

The Executive Branch

The governor is the most powerful person in the state government. A governor must be at least 30 years old. The voters in the state get to elect a governor every four years. That time is called a "term." A person can serve as governor for no more than two terms.

Here are some of the jobs the governor does. The governor:

- sees that state laws are carried out.
- suggests new laws.
- signs new laws or *vetoes* them. To veto is to turn down a law.
- makes a state budget.
- commands the state military.
- appoints judges to the state courts.
- appoints people who run departments.

A department is a group of workers who do certain jobs. There is an education department to help schools. There is a department to help farmers. Workers in other departments run state parks, work on state roads, and collect taxes. There are many departments.

Since taking office in 2001, Governor Ruth Ann Minner has worked to get things done in Delaware. She has worked for better schools, a cleaner environment, and better health care.

The Judicial Branch: The Courts

Delaware's courts decide who is right when people disagree about what a law means. Courts also decide if a person has broken the law.

Judges and juries are part of the courts. A jury is made up of 12 citizens. A jury decides if a person has broken a law or not.

Courts try to make sure that government follows its own rules. Courts try to give people a fair trial. This is called "due process" of law. It is one of our rights.

Bang! A gavel is used by a judge to start a court session.

Local Government

In some places in Delaware there are farms. In other places there are suburbs or a big city with tall buildings. Some regions have many people. Others do not. Because different places have different needs, local governments are important. Local governments are close to home. County and city governments are both local governments.

City Government

Wilmington is Delaware's only big city. Dover is our capital city, but it is not our largest city. Our state also has many large and small towns.

In each town, a mayor or city manager decides what the town needs. A group of people called a city council also help. The leaders make rules for the town. They might decide how fast people can drive on the roads. They may decide where a new store can be built. They may hire someone to run the fire department or the police department. The city council may even plan a parade and fireworks for the 4th of July!

Cities hire police workers to keep communities safe.

Levels of Government

As you have just read, there are different levels of government. You must obey the laws of all the levels. Study the chart to see how this works.

- What level includes the president of the United States?
- What level includes our governor?
- What level includes the mayor of your town or city?

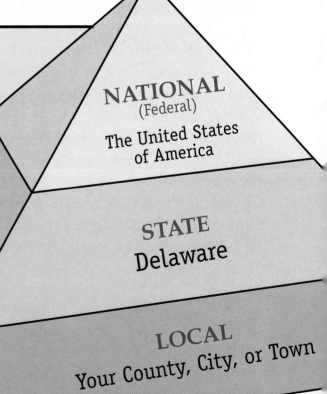

NATIONAL (Federal)
The United States of America

STATE
Delaware

LOCAL
Your County, City, or Town

County Government

Delaware is divided into three counties. Citizens elect the people who run the county government. Each county has a *county seat.* That is the town or city where the government offices are located.

There is a courthouse at the county seat. Judges and juries hear cases there. Workers in the courthouse keep copies of birth, death, and marriage certificates. If your family owns property, your county keeps a map of your property on file.

All the counties provide public libraries and parks. County governments are in charge of how land is used outside of towns and cities. New Castle County also has a county police force.

You can get a copy of your birth certificate or watch court in session at the Kent County Courthouse in Dover.

What is the county seat of Sussex County? Kent County? New Castle County? Which county do you live in?

Counties and County Seats

Wilmington

New Castle

Dover

Kent

Sussex

Georgetown

Activity

Your Local Government

You can learn about your local government. Here are some questions your class could study:

- Do you have a town or city government?
- Who is your mayor or city manager?
- Do you have a city council? What do they do?
- Where is your county courthouse?
- What kinds of offices are in your courthouse?

Government for the Nation and the State

At Your Service

The government collects tax money to pay for services people need. Government workers build and fix streets. They plow snow. They build libraries where you can check out books. Cities provide clean water. They have garbage picked up. If you play soccer on a city team or swim in a city pool, you are using a city service. Cities have parks where you can play ball and have picnics.

The government also pays for public education. If you go to a public school, your building, your books, and your teachers are paid with tax money. If you go to a private school, your parents pay for most of these things.

Some public services are provided by *volunteers*. In Delaware, many of our fire fighters and rescue workers are volunteers.

226

The Delaware Adventure

How many public services can you find in this town?

Be a Good Citizen

In our country and our state we have many rights. We must do our part to keep our freedoms. There are five major things that every adult must do to be a good citizen. Have you seen adults doing these things? Which of these things can you do right now?

1. Respect Others

No place can be a good place to live unless all the people there respect each other. This means we must try to understand each other. We should listen to each other. We should be kind. We should help others.

2. Obey the Laws

Americans choose leaders to make laws. It is our duty to obey those laws. If we believe that a law should be changed, we have the right to say what we think. Then, if enough people agree, the law will be changed.

3. Vote

Citizens who are at least 18 years old can vote for their leaders. Before they vote, they should know about the *candidates* who are running for office. A good citizen listens to what the candidates say and reads about them in newspapers. Then the voter should think hard about which candidates will be good leaders.

228

The Delaware Adventure

4. Pay Taxes

We need schools. We need paved streets. We need an army, navy, and air force to protect us. We need police workers. All of these things cost money. Governments get most of their money by taxing the people.

5. Be Willing to Serve on a Jury

Every adult citizen can be called to serve on a jury. Juries play an important role in our courts. In court, they decide if someone is guilty of a crime.

Do Your Part!

You can be a good citizen right now. To do that, you should learn about current events. Read about what the president of the United States and the governor of your state are saying and doing. If you can, visit the nation's Capitol Building in Washington, D.C., and Legislative Hall in Dover.

You will find that learning about government is fun. There is always something going on. Remember that the things government leaders do today will affect you tomorrow.

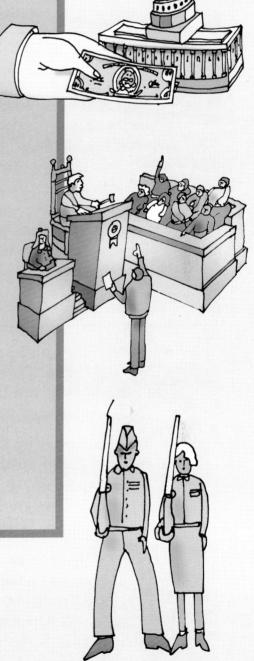

❷ MEMORY MASTER

1. What are the three branches of Delaware's government? What does each branch do?
2. What are two examples of local government that help you?
3. List at least five services that taxes help pay for.
4. Describe at least five duties of a good citizen.

From There to Here

The United States of America is among the largest countries in the world. Delaware is one of the 50 states that make up the United States. Our government is a democracy. The people rule.

The Constitution of the United States tells how our country's government is formed. It also explains the rights of the people and of the states. Delaware also has a constitution. Both the national and state constitutions divide the government into three branches. They make sure any one branch does not have all the power.

Government leaders run the government and provide services for everyone. Some of these services are paved roads, schools, and libraries.

Democracy works when all citizens do their part by respecting others, obeying the laws, voting, paying their taxes, and serving on juries.

Activity

The Preamble to the U.S. Constitution

The Constitution of the United States begins with these words:

We the people of the United States, in order to form a more perfect union, establish justice, insure domestic tranquility, provide for the common defense, promote the general welfare, and secure the blessings of liberty to ourselves and our posterity, do ordain and establish this Constitution of the United States.

What do all these big words mean? Talk about them with your class. Talk about "the blessings of liberty." Make a list on the board so you will understand the words better. Now choose one item and write or tell how your life would be different if you did not have it.

The Delaware Adventure

Activity

Discuss Current Events

At least once each week, talk with your class about current events. Collect newspaper articles about government in your town, county, state, country, and the world. Talk about what the articles mean.

Activity

Visit a Government Building

If you live close enough, visit a government building with your class or your family. Learn what goes on there. You might choose your city hall, a county courthouse, or Legislative Hall. You can arrange for someone who works in one of those places to show you around. What did you see? What did you learn? Tell your class about your trip.

Activity

Make a Government Bulletin Board

Display photographs of your governor, senators, and representatives. Learn their names. Listen for their names in the news on radio or TV. Then choose one of the leaders and learn more about him or her. You can find information on the Internet.

If it is an election year, make a bulletin board to show the people who are running for office. You can find their pictures in the newspaper. Put a star by the candidates who win the election.

"Far and away the best prize that life has to offer is the chance to work hard at work worth doing."

—*Theodore Roosevelt*

DuPont products include things you use every day. Workers at DuPont discover new ways to use chemicals to make plastic, cloth, glue, film, paint, glass, parts for cars and planes, and even rollerblades. DuPont is an important part of our economy.

Economics for Everyone

consumer
economics
employee
goods
market economy
producer
services
supply and demand

Working Together to Meet Our Needs

All people in the world need food, clothing, and a place to live. They want other things, too. Most people want a car or a bicycle to get from place to place. They want books, games, radios, and DVD players. These things are called *goods,* or products.

People also need medical care from doctors and dentists. They need education from teachers. They need to use a bank, have insurance, and get a haircut. Workers are paid to do these *services.*

Families, businesses, the community, and the government work together to provide the things people need and want.

Where did you get your last haircut? How much did you pay for the service?

It's Your Choice

A long time ago, people didn't have all the choices we have today. In colonial times, people had to build their own homes from logs and stone. They made their own clothes and grew their own vegetables and fruit. There were few books and toys.

In early times, people had a hard time getting help from a doctor because there might not be one for miles. There was no insurance. If your house burned down, no company paid to build a new one.

Times have changed. Today, we have many choices. Stores almost never run out of food, clothes, toys, and other things we want. The goods come from all over the world. We can also get many services.

Of course, people can't have everything they want. People must pay for all of their goods and services. They have to make choices, because they don't have enough money to buy everything.

Our Economy

Economics is how people make, transport, buy, and sell the goods and services they want. Just like there are many kinds of governments in the world, there are many different economic systems. In many countries, people own land and start businesses.

In other countries, the government, not the people, own all the land and all the businesses. Government leaders tell the factories what to make and what the prices will be.

In some economic systems, you can go to the doctor or the dentist for free. In our country, we pay for medical care.

When was the last time you got sick or hurt and went to a doctor? How did the doctor help you? In our economic system, doctors and nurses are usually paid by the people they help. In some economic systems in the world, they are paid by the government.

Is this man a producer or a consumer? How is producing food part of our economic system?

People and businesses work to make money called "income." A business must make a "profit." A profit is the money left over after business costs are subracted from business income. What are some costs of a grocery store?

A Market Economy

In the United States of America, we have a *market economy.* Sometimes it is called a free market economic system because anyone is free to start and own a business. Producers can make and sell whatever they think people will buy.

Employees

Business owners usually hire people to work for them. These people are called *employees.* Employees are paid for their work. They earn money to buy goods and services.

Producers and Consumers

A market economy is a careful balance between what people make to sell and what other people buy. People who make things to sell are *producers.* People who buy and use things are *consumers.*

In a strong economy, making, buying, selling, and providing services goes around and around. It helps everyone have what they want.

Supply and Demand

Consumers have a lot to say about what companies produce. When consumers buy a toy or game, they are letting producers know they should keep making that toy or game. If few people buy a certain game, companies will stop making it.

How many games should the Zoom Company make? Balancing the amount of goods a company makes with the amount people will buy is called *supply and demand.*

Price Matters

Jason wants a Zoom game for his birthday. His mother might buy it if it doesn't cost too much. The price of Zoom games will affect how many games the company sells.

However, people don't always buy goods that have the lowest price. For example, if a game becomes so popular that Zoom cannot make enough for all the children who want it, Zoom can sell the game for a higher price. Zoom thinks people will want the game so much they will be willing to pay more. The price of goods and services is affected by supply and demand.

Hoop Magic has more basketballs than consumers are willing to buy. A sale lowers the price of basketballs. At the lower price, the demand by consumers will increase.

Productive Resources

There are four things necessary to produce goods and services. These things are called productive resources. They are natural resources, capital goods, labor, and entrepreneurs.

Natural Resources

Natural resources are found in nature. They are used to produce something people want. Natural resources include plants, animals, and minerals such as iron ore. Sand, soil, and water are also natural resources. What natural resources are used to make a bicycle?

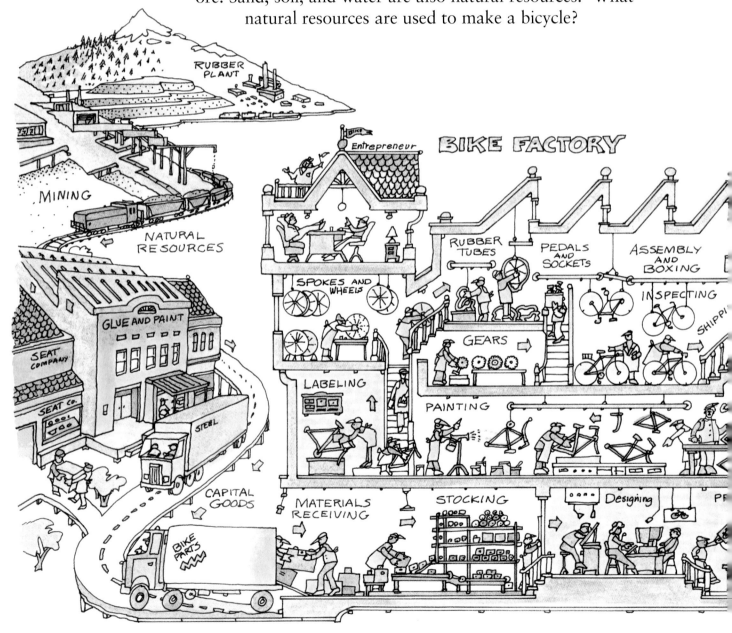

The Delaware Adventure

Capital Goods

When you use products to make other products, you are using capital goods. The hammer and nails a carpenter uses are capital goods. The tools used to make bicycles are also capital goods.

Labor

To provide goods and services, people must work. Labor means work or workers. Even when a machine does most of the work, it takes people to build the machine and run it. People work in a bicycle facotry to earn income.

Entrepreneurs

Entrepreneurs start and run new businesses. They manage natural resources, capital goods, and labor to produce goods or services. They are willing to take this risk in hopes of making a profit.

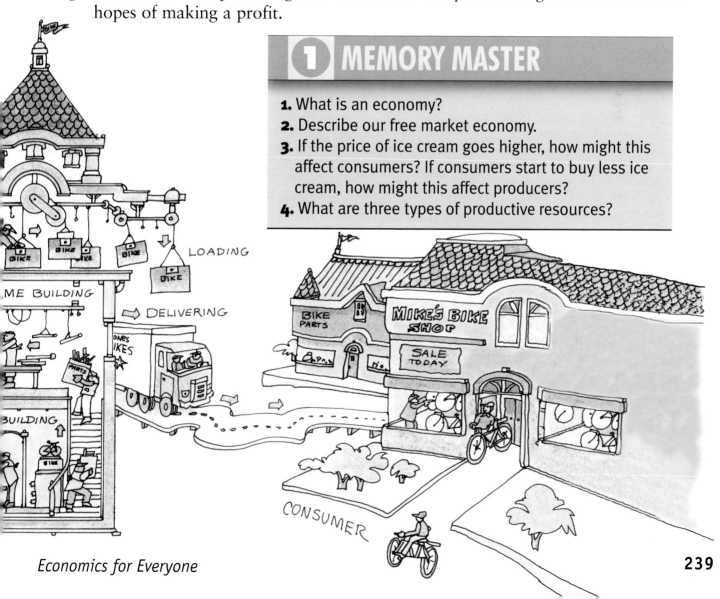

① MEMORY MASTER

1. What is an economy?
2. Describe our free market economy.
3. If the price of ice cream goes higher, how might this affect consumers? If consumers start to buy less ice cream, how might this affect producers?
4. What are three types of productive resources?

barter
export
import
technology
tourist

An amazing vehicle carries a load of heavy logs to a waiting truck or train car. Then the logs will be taken to a sawmill to be cut. The wood will be made into all kinds of things people want. Look around your room and find items made from wood. What kinds of technology helped produce the items?

Technology Improves Production

As the population grows, the economy has to be able to produce more goods and services for all the people. The people want the latest inventions to make life easier and more fun. They want better health care. They want food grown in other places. They want nice clothes that cost less. They want cars that run longer without breaking down.

To meet the demand for more goods, companies must produce more with fewer resources or find new resources. They must use the best new tools and equipment.

Technology is the science of using tools, machines, and equipment to do a job. Technology often produces more goods in less time.

Technology has resulted in newer, cheaper ways to transport goods and services. For example, a long time ago, people rode boats to get goods to market. Then they added sails and used wind power to move faster. Later, steam power moved boats. Today, gas engines give speed to boats, trains, and cars.

Technology and Prices

When more goods are produced in better ways, the cost goes down. Consumers then have more money to spend or save.

Calculators are a good example. The first calculators were large and very expensive. Then better technology improved calculators and made production faster, better, and cheaper. A company could make a lot of calculators and sell them at a lower price. Today, you probably have a small calculator you can hold in your hand. How much did it cost?

Technology Brings Change

In the 1800s, a canal was dug to join the Atlantic Ocean to Lake Erie. At first, it cost $90 per ton to ship goods from one end of the canal to the other. Ten years after the Erie Canal was built, the cost of shipping dropped. What made the cost go down?

At first, one mule walked along a dirt path beside the canal and pulled one barge. Later, better technology meant tugboats powered by steam engines pulled six or more barges at a time through the water. Goods were moved faster. They could be sold faster. The cost of shipping went down.

Year	Cost of Shipping
1825 (before canal)	$90 per ton
1835 (after canal)	$ 4 per ton

A modern ocean vehicle moves cars and other heavy items from where they are made to where they are sold. Why is it often better to transport heavy goods by water than across land?

Change over Time

Economic systems change over time. Do you remember how Native Americans and early settlers **bartered** for what they wanted? They traded what they had for what other people had. A child who lived along the coast might wear a copper bracelet made in a faraway place. A child who lived a long way from the ocean might wear a necklace of shells. An Indian father traded a pile of soft beaver fur for a metal cooking pot or a metal knife.

At one time, wampum, nails, tobacco, and fur were used like money. They had a lot of value. However, there were arguments over the value of goods. A person might think his cow was worth a lot more than bags of potatoes. If farmers grew too much tobacco, its value went down.

Paper money and gold or silver coins solved some of these problems. They were easy to carry around and lasted a long time. Making change was easier. The value of money, however, still changes today.

How does money change value? Ask some adults how much a dollar bought 25 years ago. How much does it buy today? Then ask what a dime bought a long time ago. What can you buy with a dime today?

American Indians and Europeans bartered for what they wanted. Can you imagine trapping animals and trading their fur when you wanted tools, cloth, or jewelry?

The Delaware Adventure

Why Do People Use Money?

Today, people are willing to accept paper money and coins in exchange for goods and services. Families have to decide how to use their money to pay for all the things they want. They should also save some money to use later for emergencies and expensive things such as a house, a car, or a college education. They must pay taxes to the government.

How do the adults you live with get money? Do they produce or sell goods or services? How do they spend their money? Do they save money?

Banks Help a Community

Checking accounts and savings accounts are only one way banks help families and the community. Banks also make loans for homes and cars. Businesses often borrow money for buildings, machines, and supplies. Then the business can produce more.

When businesses grow, they hire more people. The people earn more income, spend more on goods and services, and may put more money into savings. Now banks have even more money to loan. Banks also pay taxes.

Banks and other financial institutions loan money to buy homes. Loans are important because most people don't have the thousands of dollars it takes to buy a home. It takes many years to pay back the loan.

*Adults can put their money into a **checking account**. They can pay for things with checks as long as there is enough money in their account.*

*Anyone can put money into a **savings account**. They can take out the money at any time.*

How Does Government Affect the Economy?

Almost 100 years ago, T. Coleman du Pont wanted to build a road from Selbyville to Wilmington. He used his own money to pay for building the DuPont Highway. Today it is Route 13 from Wilmington to Dover and Route 113 from Dover to Selbyville. Later, the road was given to the state of Delaware.

Today, governments hire businesses to build highways. They make moving goods cheaper and faster. Governments also pay for our army and navy, police and fire protection, state parks, public libraries, and education.

Governments pay workers in these businesses with money from taxes. In most other states, when you buy clothes, toys, or food, you pay a sales tax. Delaware does not have a sales tax. Instead, people and businesses pay taxes on their income and on their property.

Firefighters are hired and paid by the government. Where does the government get the money to pay firefighters?

Sharing with the World

Today's technology allows people to communicate quickly and cheaply. Satellites, cell phones, computers, and the Internet link countries around the world.

With modern communication, people can learn more about other places. They can do business in other countries. When your mother orders a product on the phone, she doesn't know if the person she is talking to lives in your town or in India or China. People around the world are helping each other get the goods and services they want.

Phone calls, music, and television programs are often sent over air waves by satellites. They orbit in the sky high above the earth. Satellite dishes receive the signals.

Ground Transportation

Transportation means moving goods and people from one place to another. This is very important for business. How does it make life better for everyone?

Roads are an important part of transportation. The first roads were trails the American Indians made through the woods. Over time, wagons used some of the trails. This meant farmers could get their goods to market more easily and in less time.

Much later, roads were paved for cars. Building roads has never stopped. Today, modern highways such as I-95 and Routes 1 and 13 connect Delaware's businesses to the rest of the nation.

Railroads are also an important way of moving people and goods. Throngs of men and women ride the Amtrak line to get to work each day. The CSX and Norfolk Southern lines haul Delaware's farm goods, chemicals, automobiles, and other manufactured goods to seaports, factories, and stores.

Large ships are pulled into the harbor by small tugboats. Can you see the tugboat?

Waterways

Delaware's location on the Delmarva Peninsula has helped its economy grow. It is surrounded by the Delaware and Chesapeake Bays and the Atlantic Ocean.

Ships reach the Atlantic Ocean in two ways. The ships travel on the Delaware River to Cape Henlopen to reach the ocean. Ships also travel through the C&D Canal to reach the Chesapeake Bay and then move into the Atlantic Ocean.

Port of Wilmington

The Port of Wilmington is the busiest port on the Delaware River. It receives more bananas and other fresh fruit than any other seaport in the world!

Study the chart to see what products are **imported** (shipped in) from other countries and what products are **exported** (shipped out) to other countries from the United States. Hundreds of ships bring the goods in and out of the port.

How does shipping goods in and out of other countries improve the lives of people in many places? If all shipping stopped for some reason, what would you miss the most?

IMPORTED PRODUCTS	Imported From:	Shipped To:
Bananas, Grapes, Plums, Apples, Pears, Clementines	Belize, Costa Rica, Brazil, Chile, Morocco	Eastern United States, Canada
Frozen Hamburger Meat (for Wendy's, McDonalds, Burger King), Lamb, Fish	New Zealand, Australia	United States, Canada
Frozen Orange, Apple, and Pear Juice Concentrate	Brazil, Belize, Argentina, Costa Rica	United States
Lumber, Wood Products	Canada, Sweden	United States
Automobiles: Audi, Volkswagon	Germany, Mexico, Brazil	United States
Salts, Sodium Nitrate	United States, Chile	United States, Canada
Steel	various countries	Eastern United States
Petroleum Products	Canada, Saudi Arabia, Mexico, Nigeria, others	Eastern United States

EXPORTED PRODUCTS	Exported From:	Shipped To:
Automobiles: General Motors	United States	Middle East
Automobiles: Previously Owned	United States	Central America

The Delaware Adventure

Where Do People Work?

You have already learned that people earn money by working at jobs or running a business. There are many kinds of jobs.

Agriculture

Delaware's farmland makes up a little more than one-third of the state's land. Sussex County produces more poultry than any other county in the United States. Delaware's other farm products include milk, vegetables, corn, flowers and trees for yards, soybeans, and grains. Farming and distributing food takes a lot of workers.

Private Companies

Thousands of people in our state work for large and small businesses. They manufacture products such as chemicals and automobiles. They work in banks and offices. People work in health care. Other people work selling goods.

Delaware's 15 Largest Private Employers
Bank of America
E.I. DuPont de Nemours & Co.
Christiana Care Health System
JPMorgan Chase & Company
AstraZeneca
Wal-Mart Stores
Mountaire Farms of Delmarva
Perdue Farms
Bayhealth Medical Center
Alfred I. DuPont Institute
Wilmington Trust
Happy Harry's
DaimlerChrysler
Acme Markets
Integrity Staffing Solutions

Workers earn money by making cars in this factory in Newark. They will sell them to people in many cities. It takes a lot of skill to help make a car that will go safely for thousands of miles.

Economics for Everyone

Government Jobs

People in our state also work for the government. They work for schools, highway departments, libraries, police departments, emergency services, the court system, and the military.

Tourism

Each year thousands of *tourists* visit Delaware. They come to visit beaches, museums, and historical sites. They come to shop in outlet stores. They eat in restaurants and attend local events and festivals. They buy gas for cars or ride trains and buses. Some stay overnight in hotels.

Many workers in our state provide services for tourists. That is the way these workers make money. When tourists spend money they are part of a major industry called tourism. Tourism is an important industry.

Delaware's Largest Government Employers

State of Delaware
Dover Air Force Base
County Governments
University of Delaware

Away it goes! The International Punkin Chunkin Contest is held each fall in Nassau. The idea is to make the machine that will throw a pumpkin the farthest. In 2005 the event brought about 20,000 people.

The Delaware Adventure

Tourists and local people flock to the beach to swim, soak up the sun, and feel the thrill of a fish on the line.

2 MEMORY MASTER

1. What does money do in an economy?
2. How do banks affect a community?
3. How do transportation and communication affect the way we live?
4. How does the Port of Wilmington connect Delaware with the world?
5. Name five jobs or businesses in Delaware.

Activity

We Are All Connected

Our market economy is made up of consumers and producers. Producers use productive resources to make and sell what consumers want. Workers earn money and use it to buy the goods and services they want.

Draw a large picture to show the people and businesses in this story. On your picture:

- Use arrows to connect the people and businesses.
- Each time there is a money exchange, draw a dollar sign ($) on the arrow.
- Label items in the picture with an "R" for production resources, "G" for goods, and "S" for services.

As a class, answer these questions:

1. What are some of the businesses in this community?
2. What resources do these businesses buy?
3. What goods and services do they sell?
4. Who are the consumers?
5. How do these people earn money?
6. If Mrs. Lopez closed her restaurant, how might consumers and other businesses in the community be affected?

Burger Haven Helps the Economy

Mrs. Lopez owns a restaurant called Burger Haven. She hires Jeff Nast to work as a chef.

After work, Jeff uses some of his income to buy new scuba diving equipment from a store called Diver Down. The owner of Diver Down then uses the money he gets from Jeff and other customers to pay his employee, Ms. Waters.

Ms. Waters uses some of the money she earns to take her family to a concert at Symphony Hall and to dinner at the Corner Café.

At the same time, Mrs. Lopez uses some of the money from her customers at Burger Haven to buy new ovens from Ovens Unlimited. Business has been good for Ovens Unlimited. The owners decide to take out a loan from a bank and build a second factory. They can hire more workers and make more ovens.

Technology  Tie-In

In this chapter you learned about using technology to produce products faster and better. Try this experiment. See how many math problems you can do without a calculator in 5 minutes. How many answers were correct?

Now do the same math problems in 5 minutes using a calculator. How did the use of technology (the calculator) affect the amount and accuracy of math problems you solved?

Geography 🌍 Tie-In

On a world map in your classroom, locate the countries that export and import goods at the Port of Wilmington. Label each country with a sticky note and connect it with a piece of yarn to the Port of Wilmington. The chart on page 246 will help you complete this map.

As a class, talk about how international trade links Delaware with the rest of the world. How might international trade create jobs for people in Delaware? How might international trade be good for consumers in Delaware and other parts of the world?

Activity

Money Matters

Money is not as simple as you might think! Talk to an adult to learn more about two or three of these words and then tell your class what you learned. Take some written notes or draw some pictures to share what you learn. Or, you could make a book about money, with one page for each word on the list.

- Interest
- Profit
- Credit Card
- Checking Account
- Budget
- Banks
- Debit Card
- Savings Account
- Loans

The United States of America

Pacific Ocean

★ Olympia
Washington

★ Salem
Oregon

★ Helena
Montana

North Dakota
★ Bismarck

★ Boise
Idaho

South Dakota
Pierre ★

Wyoming

Cheyenne ★

Sacramento ★
★ Carson City
Nevada

Salt Lake City ★
Utah

Denver ★
Colorado

Nebraska

Lincoln ★

California

★ Santa Fe

Arizona
New Mexico

★ Phoenix

Kansas

Tope

Oklahoma
★
Oklahoma City

0 ——— 500 Miles

Alaska
Juneau ★

0 ——— 100 Miles
Hawaii
Honolulu ★

Texas

Austin ★

MEXICO

The Delaware Adventure

CANADA

Minnesota

Paul

Wisconsin

Madison ★

Michigan

Lansing ★

Iowa

es Moines ★

Illinois

Springfield ★

Indianapolis ★

Indiana

Ohio

Columbus ★

Missouri

Jefferson City ★

Kentucky

Frankfort ★

West Virginia

Charleston ★

Vermont
Montpelier

Maine

Augusta ★

New Hampshire
Concord

New York

Albany ★

Massachusetts
Boston

Rhode Island
Providence

Pennsylvania

Harrisburg ★

Connecticut
Hartford

New Jersey
Trenton

Delaware
Dover

Maryland
Annapolis

Washington D.C.

Richmond ★

Virginia

Raleigh ★

North Carolina

Arkansas

Little Rock ★

Nashville ★

Tennessee

Columbia ★

South Carolina

Atlanta ★

Alabama

Georgia

Atlantic
Ocean

N

W   E

S

Louisiana

Jackson ★

Montgomery ★

Mississippi

Baton Rouge ★

Tallahassee ★

0   500 Miles

Gulf of Mexico

Florida

THE BAHAMAS

Maps

Maps

253

The World

Arctic Ocean

Greenland

Beaufort Sea

Alaska (U.S.)

Bering Sea

Gulf of Alaska

Hudson Bay

Canada

North America

United States of America

Atlantic Ocean

Canary Islands

Western Sahara

Mauritania

Senegal

Gambia

Guinea Bissau

Sierra Leone

Liberi

Mexico

Gulf of Mexico

Caribbean Sea

Venezuela

Colombia

Ecuador

Guyana

Suriname

French Guiana

Equator

Peru

Bolivia

Brazil

South America

Paraguay

Atlantic Ocean

Chile

Argentina

Uruguay

Pacific Ocean

N

W   E

S

Falkland Islands (U.K.)

Inset: Caribbean

United States

Gulf of Mexico

Bahamas

Atlantic Ocean

Cuba

Mexico

Dominican Republic

Puerto Rico (U.S.)

Haiti

Belize

Jamaica

Guatemala

Honduras

Caribbean Sea

El Salvador

Nicaragua

Trinidad

Costa Rica

Panama

Venezuela

Colombia

Pacific Ocean

Hawaii (U.S.)

Inset: Europe

North Sea

Estonia

Latvia

Russia

Denmark

Lithuania

Russia

Ireland

Netherlands

Belarus

United Kingdom

Poland

Belgium

Germany

Atlantic Ocean

Liechtenstien

France

Switzerland

Czech Republic

Slovakia

Ukraine

Austria

Hungary

Moldova

Slovenia

Romania

Croatia

Bosnia

Portugal

Spain

Balearic Islands (Sp.)

Corsica (Fr.)

Italy

Sardinia (It.)

Macedonia

Yugoslavia

Bulgaria

Black Sea

Albania

Greece

Turkey

Mediterranean Sea

Sicily (It.)

Country Abbreviations	
Fr.	France
It.	Italy
Sp.	Spain
U.E.A.	United Arab Emirates
U.K.	United Kingdom
U.S.	United States

The Delaware Adventure

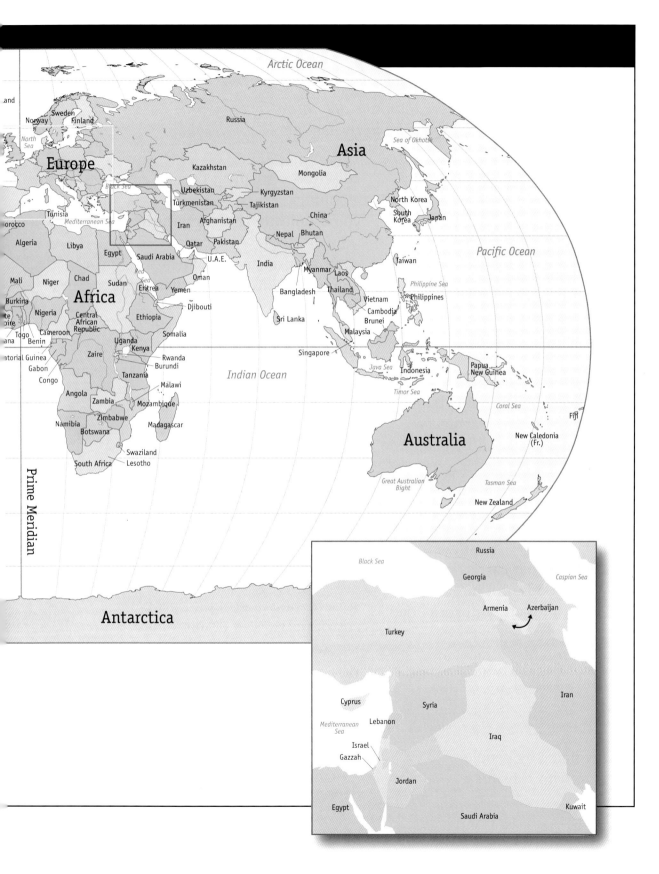

Arctic Ocean

Norway
Sweden
Finland

.and

North
Sea

Russia

Asia

Sea of Okhotsk

Europe

Kazakhstan

Mongolia

Black Sea

Uzbekistan

Kyrgyzstan

North Korea

orocco

Turkmenistan

Tajikistan

South
Korea

Japan

Tunisia

Mediterranean Sea

Iran

Afghanistan

China

Pacific Ocean

Algeria

Libya

Egypt

Qatar

Pakistan

Nepal

Bhutan

Saudi Arabia

U.A.E.

India

Taiwan

Mali

Niger

Chad

Sudan

Red
Sea

Oman

Myanmar

Laos

Philippine Sea

Burkina

Africa

Eritrea

Yemen

Bangladesh

Thailand

Philippines

Nigeria

Central
African
Republic

Djibouti

Sri Lanka

Vietnam
Cambodia

te
oire

Ethiopia

Brunei

Togo
Benin

Cameroon

Somalia

Malaysia

atorial Guinea

Zaire

Uganda
Kenya

Singapore

Gabon

Rwanda
Burundi

Indian Ocean

Java Sea

Indonesia

Papua
New Guinea

Congo

Tanzania

Angola

Malawi

Timor Sea

Coral Sea

Zambia

Mozambique

Namibia

Zimbabwe

Fiji

Botswana

Madagascar

New Caledonia
(Fr.)

Australia

Swaziland

South Africa

Lesotho

Great Australian
Bight

Tasman Sea

Prime Meridian

New Zealand

Antarctica

Russia

Black Sea

Georgia

Caspian Sea

Armenia

Azerbaijan

Turkey

Iran

Cyprus

Syria

Mediterranean
Sea

Lebanon

Israel

Iraq

Gazzah

Jordan

Egypt

Saudi Arabia

Kuwait

Maps

255

Glossary

Words often have more than one definition. These words are defined as they are used in the lessons of this book.

A

abolish: to end

abolitionist: one who works to end slavery

adobe: brick made from clay mixed with straw and dried in the sun

allies: countries that help each other during war

amendment: a change or addition to a constitution

ancestor: a relative who lived before you

archaeology: the science of learning about people of the past by studying artifacts

artifact: something made or used by people long ago

astronaut: a person who goes into space

B

barge: a large, flat boat that carries goods

barter: to trade with goods, not money

bola: a weapon of long cords with rocks tied on the ends

bombardment: to constantly attack

budget: a written plan for spending money

C

canal: a waterway made by people

candidate: a person who runs for a government office

colony: a settlement or land ruled by another country

communicate: to share information back and forth

compromise: an agreement where each side gives in a little so an agreement can be made

confidence: faith in yourself

conquer: to take over and rule

constitution: the written rules and plan of government

consumer: a person who buys and uses goods and services

convert: to persuade a person to change to a different religion

county seat: the town where government offices are located

cradleboard: a board covered with soft animal skins used for an American Indian baby

culture: how a group of people live

customs: ways of doing things

D

defeat: to win victory over; to cause to lose

delegate: a representative

democracy: rule by the people; rule by the majority

depression: a time when a lot of people can't make enough money to live on

dictator: a ruler who has all the power

discrimination: when people treat other people badly solely on the basis of race, etc.

dispute: a disagreement

distribution: to get goods to the people who want them

document: an official paper

dynamite: an explosive

E

economics: the study of how groups make, transport, buy, and sell goods and services

edible: fit to be eaten

editor: one who gets articles or books ready to publish

emancipate: to free

employee: a person who works for someone else for wages

environment: natural physical and human surroundings, including land, water, air, buildings, etc

export: to ship goods out of a country

extinct: no longer living anywhere on the earth

F–G

famine: an extreme scarcity of food over a long time

federal: national; government for all the states

freight: transported goods

fugitive: one who is running from the law

geography: the study of where and how people live in the world

goods: products made, bought, and sold

graffiti: messy, illegal writing or painting on public property

grid: evenly spaced, crossing lines on a map used to locate a place

H

hemisphere: half of the planet Earth

Hispanic: from a Spanish-speaking country

humid: having moist air

hunter-gatherer: a person who gets food by hunting wild animals and gathering wild plants

I

illegal: against the law

immigrant: a person who moves into a country to live

import: to bring goods into a country

indivisible: not able to be divided

integration: opposite of segregation; when people of all races participate together at work, school, in the military, etc.

invade: to come in and take over

inventor: a person who designs or makes something that did not exist before

L

labor union: a group of workers who unite to solve problems on the job

latitude: imaginary lines that run east and west on a globe or map

Glossary 257

legend: a story that explains how things came to be; a story told out loud from memory

legislature: a group who is elected to make the laws

locate: to find

lock: a method of raising or lowering boats in a canal

longitude: imaginary lines that run north and south on a globe or map

M

manufacturing: producing goods from raw materials

market economy: an economic system where anyone is free to start and run a business

merchant: a person who buys, sells, and ships goods to make money; a store owner

militia: a group of men who join together to protect their property

miserable: very uncomfortable or sad

moccasin: Native American footwear made of animal skins

mutiny: to revolt against the captain of a ship

N-O

native: being born in a place; being naturally from a place

nomad: a person who travels from place to place to find food and shelter

oppose: to work against

orchard: a field of fruit trees

P

paddle wheel: a large wheel with flat blades that pulls a boat through the water

parachute: a device that slows down a person falling from a plane

paved: roads covered with hard material

peninsula: a large area of land that is surrounded by water on three sides

plantation: a very large farm

pollute: to make air, land, or water dirty and unsafe

population: the total number of people in a place

powwow: an American Indian celebration of food, dancing, and singing

preserve: to keep

produce: to make

R

ratify: to officially approve

rebellion: an armed fight against your own government or leaders

Reconstruction: a time of rebuilding the country after the Civil War

refuse: to turn down

regiment: an official group of soldiers who belong to the same unit

region: a place that has features that are alike in some way

representative: a person elected to vote on behalf of other people; a person elected to help make laws

rescue: to free from danger or evil

revolution: when people fight to overthrow their own government

The Delaware Adventure

rival: a person or country who tries to be better or stronger

rural: having to do with the country or farm

S

satellite: a device that orbits in space and sends information to Earth

secede: to have part of a country break away

segregation: separating people by race

services: in economics, work done for people in order to earn money

sinew: a tendon that connects muscle and bones

soot: fine black dust that comes from burning coal

stockade: strong, tall, log fence

strike: when workers agree to stop working until they get more pay or other benefits such as a safer workplace

submarine: a boat that travels under the water

suburb: a community of houses, schools, and stores next to a larger city

supply and demand: a balance between making enough, too little, or too much of what people are willing to buy

surrender: in war, to give up to the other side

survey: an official measurement of the land

T

tax: money people must pay to the government

technology: the science of using tools, machines, and electronics to produce goods

tenant farmer: a farmer who works land owned by another and pays with part of the crop

terrorism: acts of violence and destruction

toll: a fee paid to use a turnpike

tourist: a person who takes a tour or visits a place for pleasure

troops: soldiers or groups of soldiers

turnpike: a road that people have to pay to use

U–V–W

urban: having to do with the city instead of the country

vehicle: a car, truck, bus, or other means of motorized transportation

veto: to say "No" to stop a bill from becoming a law

volunteers: a person who works for others without pay

wampum: tiny shells that were strung like beads and used as money or as a sign of trust

Glossary

Index

A

Abolitionists, 135
Addams, Jane, 180
Africa, 49, 50, 58
African Americans, 105, 121, 136, 149, 156, 157, 181, 192, 208
African Methodist Episcopal Church, 137
Agriculture, *See* Farming
Alfred I. DuPont Hospital for Children, 167
Allegany Mountains, 30
Allen, Richard, 137
American Indians, *See* Native Americans and specific tribes
American Revolution, 84–94, 134, 218
Amtrak, 245
Anasazi Indians, 27, 28
Appalachian Mountains, 14, 29, 78
Archaeology, 41
Archaic Indians, 25
Asbury, Francis, 112
Asia, 48, 49–50, 201 205, 211
Atlantic Coastal Plain Region, 12–13
Atlantic flyway, 13
Atlantic Ocean, 11, 12, 13, 48, 49, 78, 245
Automobiles, 184, 193–194

B

Babiarz, Mary, 164, 174
Bancroft Mills, 175
Barratt's Chapel, 112
Bassett, Richard, 96
Battle of Brandywine, 93
Bedford, Gunning, Jr., 96
Bell, Alexander Graham, 183
Bethany Beach, 172
Big August Quarterly, 137
Bill of Rights, 99, 219, 220–221, 222
Black Anthony, 58
Blacks, *See* African Americans
Blocksoms Colored School, 156
Blue Hens, 90
Bombay Hook National Wildlife Refuge, 17
Booth, John Wilkes, 154
Boston, 53, 82
Branches of Government, 98–99, 218, 222–223
Brandywine Creek State Park, 16
Brandywine River, 3, 72, 92, 125-128
Brandywine Springs Park, 184
Broom, Jacob, 96
Bush, George W., 210

C

Cahokia, 29
California, 109
Canada, 79, 80, 136
Cannon, Patty, 138
Cape Henlopen, 12, 13, 54, 202
Carothers, Wallace, 198
Catholic Church/Catholics, 49, 50, 105
Cedar Creek, 118
Charles II, King, 61
Cheney, Edward, 167
Chesapeake and Delaware Canal, 120-121, 207, 245
Chesapeake Bay, 32, 91, 138
Child labor, 176–177, 179
China/Chinese, 51, 117, 168
Christina River, 69, 168, 201
Christina, Queen, 57
Church of England, 52, 60
Citro, Angelo, 165
Civil Rights Movement, 208–209
Civil War, 132–159
Clark, Lydia, 39
Clarke, Aletta, 118
Clayton, 123
Cold War, 203
Columbus, Christopher, 49, 50
Concord, 84
Confederacy, 144–146, 149, 152–155
Congress (U.S.), 97, 99, 220
Connor, James P., 203
Constitution (Delaware State), 87, 104–105, 222
Constitution (U.S.), 94, 97, 218, 222, 230
Constitutional Convention, 96

Continental Congress, 83, 84
Cooch's Bridge, 91
Counties, 225
Courts, 87, 221, 223, 229
Crockett, Davy, 122

D

Davis, Samuel Boyer, 106
De La Warr, Lord, 56
Declaration of Independence, 84–85, 218
Delaware Bay, 11, 32, 92, 107, 246
Delaware City, 17, 114
Delaware Colony, 72
Delaware Continentals, 89
Delaware Day, 98
Delaware Declaration of Rights, 76
Delaware Hosiery Mill, 174
Delaware Memorial Bridge, 207
Delaware Railroad, 123
Delaware River, 17, 56, 70, 90, 114, 119, 120, 246
Delmarva Peninsula, 8, 9
Democracy, 216
DeVries, David, 56

Dewey Beach, 172
Dickinson Plantation, 68-69
Dickinson, John, 68, 81, 96, 135
Dickinson, Samuel, 68
Dinah, 69
Dixon, Jeremiah, 64
Dover Air Force Base, 202

Dover, 15, 69, 87, 92, 98, 104, 123, 193
Du Pont Powder Mills/Yards, 126, 127, 151, 166
du Pont, Alfred I, 167
du Pont, E.I., 126
du Pont, Lammot, 151
du Pont, Pierre S., 196
du Pont, T. Coleman, 193, 244
Duke of York, 59
DuPont Company, 102, 193, 195, 198
DuPont Highway, 193-194, 207, 244
Dutch, 51, 54-57

E

Eastern Woodland Indians, 27, 30
Edison, Thomas, 183
Education, *See* schools
Electricity, 182–183, 191
Ellis Island, 163-165
Emancipation Proclamation, 150, 154
Emigrants, *See* immigrants
England/English, 52–53, 60–63, 70, 79-85, 106, 122, 124
Europe/Europeans, 48–51, 163, 195, 201
Evans, Oliver, 124, 125
Evans, Sarah, 157

F

Farming, 15, 17, 37, 65–68, 88, 110–111, 191, 194, 247
Finland/Finns, 57
First State, 98
Fort Christina, 57, 58
Fort Delaware, 153
Fort Miles, 202
Fort Sumter, 145
France/French, 50, 79, 106, 163, 195
Franklin, Benjamin, 94
Frazer, William, 110
Frederica, 112
Frederica, 204
Freedmen's Bureau, 156
Fugitive Slave Law, 142

G

Garrett, Thomas, 140
General Assembly, 62, 87, 88, 92, 104, 222
George III, King, 80, 87, 89
Georgetown Colored School, 196
Georgetown, 157, 193
Germany/Germans, 109, 162, 164, 165, 195, 203
Gettysburg, 152
Gilpin Paper Mills, 127
Gilpin, Thomas and Joshua, 127
Glasgow, 91
Government, Delaware, 98
Government, Federal, 95–99, 216

Government, Local, 224
Great Compromise, 97
Great Depression, 199
Greenwood, 179

H

Hagley Museum, 124, 127, 151
Hanson, Nancy, 93
Harlan and Hollingsworth, 175
Harrington, 123
Hawaii, 5, 200
Hilles, Florence Bayard, 197
Hispanics, 211
Hockessin, 111
Holland, 51
House of Representatives, 97
Howe, Lord William, 89-92
Hudson, Henry, 51
Hull House, 180

I

Ice Age, 24
Immigrants, 162–165, *See also*
    specific groups
Indentured servants, 67
India, 211
Indians, *See* Native Americans
    and specific tribes
Industrial Revolution, 124
Ireland/Irish, 109, 121
Iron Hill, 24
Italy/Italian, 50, 162, 165

J

James, Duke of York, 62, 64
Jamestown, 52
Japan/Japanese, 200, 203, 211

Jefferson, Thomas, 85, 108,
    126, 218
Jewish/Jews, 105, 162, 165
Jim Crow Laws, 181
Jones, Absalom, 137
Jones, Bessie, 183
Jones, Jacob, 107

K

Kennedy, John F., 204
Kent County, 62, 68, 136, 225
King, Martin Luther Jr., 209
Knights of Labor, 178
Korean War, 205

L

Labor Day, 178
Labor Unions, 178
Laurel, 123
Legend, 42
Lenni Lenape Indians, 32–36
Lewes, 13, 62, 63, 69, 106–107,
    119
Lexington, 84
Lincoln, Abraham, 143–146,
    150, 154, 155
Louisiana Purchase/Territory,
    108

M

Manufacturing, 102–103, 109,
    124–129, 168, 174–179
Marvil, Joshua H., 169
Maryland, 37, 65, 66, 134, 141,
    144
Mason, Charles, 64
Massachusetts, 52, 53, 82, 89,
    149

McKean, Thomas, 80, 83, 86
McKinly, Dr. John, 92
Methodist Church, 112, 113,
    135, 137, 172
Mexico/Mexicans, 50, 108, 211
Middle East, 210
Middletown, 24, 123
Mifflin, Warner, 136
Milford, 149, 202
Millsboro, 43
Minuit, Peter, 57, 58
Mississippi River, 29, 108
Mitchell, Littleton, 202
Montgomery, Betsy, 99
Mound Builders, 27, 29

N

Nanticoke Indians, 32, 37–40,
    43
Nanticoke River, 138
Native Americans, 22–45, 50,
    51, 53, 63, 73, 75, 79, 242,
    See also specific tribes
Netherlands, 51, 54
New Amstel, 59
New Amsterdam, 59
New Castle and Frenchtown
    Railroad, 122
New Castle Army Base, 202
New Castle, 59, 63, 64, 69, 79,
    84, 92
New Deal, 199
New Jersey, 54, 90
New Netherland, 54, 59
New Sweden, 47, 57-59
New York/City, 32, 54, 58, 59,
    89, 91, 114, 210
Newark Academy, 69

Newark, 69, 91, 206
Newport, 116, 125
Nineteenth Amendment, 197
North Korea, 205
Nylon, 198

O

Oak Orchard, 39
Oil, 17
Old Swedes Lutheran
    Church, 69, 71
Oregon Country, 108
Oregon, 109
Owen, William, 149

P–Q

Pakistan, 211
Paleo Indians, 24
Parliament, 80, 81
Peaches, 169–170
Pearl Harbor, 200
Penn, William, 60–64, 75
Pennsylvania, 32, 78, 90–91,
    142, 149
Peoples Settlement House,
    180
Philadelphia, 70, 83, 84, 86,
    91, 92, 94, 96, 116, 118
Philadelphia, Wilmington,
    and Baltimore Railroad,
    123
Pickett's Charge, 152
Piedmont Region, 14
Pilgrims, 52
Pledge of Allegiance, 144
Plymouth, 52
Poland/Polish, 162, 164

Pollution, 17
Population, 21, 109, 131,
    187
Port of Wilmington, 246
Printz, Johan, 58
Protestants, 105
Puerto Rico, 211
Puritans, 53
Pyle, Sarah Webb, 180
Quakers, 60–63, 70, 135,
    136, 137, 140

R

Railroads, 122–123, 168,
    172, 190-192
Read, George, 83, 86, 92, 96
Reconstruction, 155
Redding, Louis, 209
Reeves, Isaac, 114
Rehoboth Beach, 13, 172,
    173, 211, 249
Reliance, 138
Revolutionary War, 91, *See
    also* American Revolution
Reybold, Philip, 114
Richardson and Robbins
    Cannery, 170
Richardson, Alden, 170
Robbins, James, 170
Rocky Mountains, 108
Rodney, Caesar, 80, 83, 86,
    115, 135
Rodney, Thomas, 90
Roosevelt, Franklin D., 199
Russia/Russians, 162, 165,
    195

S

Saint Augustine, 50
Saudi Arabia, 17
Schools, 113, 156–157, 196,
    208, 200
Scots-Irish, 69
Seaford, 123, 198
Seaside Nature Park, 12
Selbyville, 193, 244
Semple, Anna, 146
Senate, U.S., 97
Separation Day, 84
September 11, 2001, 210
Shadd, Mary Ann, 136
Shipley, Elizabeth, 70
Shipley, William, 70
Slavery, 65–66, 68, 69, 71,
    87, 105, 134–144, 150,
    155
South America, 17
South Carolina, 144, 145
South Korea, 205, 211
Soviet Union, 203, 204
Spain/Spanish, 49, 50
Spencer, Peter, 113, 137
Springer, Carl, 46, 71
Springer, Thomas, 111
St. Jones River, 68
Stamp Act, 80
State Seal, viii, 88
State Symbols, viii-ix
Statue of Liberty, 163
Steamboats, 118, 119, 121,
    128
Steele, Cecile, 194
Stowe, Harriet Beecher, 159
Strawberries, 171, 176–177

Stuart, Mary Ann Sorden, 179
Stuyvesant, Peter, 59
Sussex County, 39, 62, 171, 194, 247
Sweden/Swedish, 57–59

T

Taxes, 80–82, 95, 105, 229
Telegraph, 173
Tennessee, 122, 197
Thirteenth Amendment, 155
Thompson, Mary Wilson, 197
Topkis, Sally, 165
Tourism, 248
Townsend, John Jr., 173
Trade, 49
Trains, *See* Railroad
Trap Pond State Park, 13
Triangular trade, 70–71
Tubman, Harriet, 140, 141
Tuskegee Airmen, 202

U–V

U.S. Supreme Court, 209
Underground Railroad, 139, 140
Union, 144, 145-147, 152–154
Vespucci, Amerigo, 50
Vietnam War, 205
Virginia, 52, 66, 85, 94, 138
Voting, 105, 179, 197, 221

W

Wampum, 39
War of 1812, 106–108, 126
Washington, D.C., 13, 154, 209, 210
Washington, George, 79, 84, 89–94, 95, 96, 99

West End Reading Room, 180
Wilmington Friends School, 69
Wilmington, 14, 69, 70, 92, 93, 109, 116, 119, 128–129, 136, 150, 165, 166, 183, 206, 224
Women's rights, 179, 197
World War I, 195
World War II, 200–203, 207

Y–Z

Yorktown, 94
Zwaanendael, 54–55

Image Credits

Prelims: iii SS/Evgeny E. Kuklev, iv–v HSD, vi–vii GR. **Chapter One:** 2-3 Tom Till, 4 (bottom) SS/Joy Fera, 5 (top) Susan Myers, (bottom) SS/Denis Pepin, 12 iStock/Andrei Tchernov, 13 DTO, 14 (top) SS/Natalia Bratslavsky, (bottom) ericcrossan.com, 15 (top) DTO, (bottom) PTG/Michael Long, 16 (top) Jerry Irwin, (center) SS/Maria Yfanti, 17 U.S. Fish & Wildlife Service: Digital Library System, 19 iStock/James Bowers. **Chapter Two:** 22-23 Illinois Historic Preservation Agency, 24 (top) SS/Michele Bagdon, 25 (top) Burke Museum University of Washington/Joyce Bergan, (right) DHCA, 26 (top) Illustration by John T. Kraft; Courtesy of Lenape Lifeways, Inc., (center) Janis J. Hansen, (bottom) GR, 28 (left) Arizona State Museum, (bottom) Kindra Clineff, 29 Cahokia Mounds State Historic Site, 30 (top) GR, (center) Tara Prindle, Native Tech, (bottom) DHCA, 31 Courtesy of the National Archives of Canada, 32 GR, 34 Illustration by John T. Kraft; Courtesy of Lenape Lifeways, Inc., 35 GR, 36 (center) LOC, (bottom) Nebraska State Historical Society, Museum of Nebraska History Collections, 38 Minnesota Historical Society, 39 (top) Pocumtuck Valley Memorial Association, Memorial Hall Museum, Deerfield, Massachusetts, (bottom) Delaware Public Archives, 40 GR, 41 (left) SS/Krzysztof Nieciecki, 42 GR, 43 Kevin Fleming/CORBIS.

Chapter Three: 46–47 Robert E. Goodier, A.W.S., W.H.S, Courtesy of PNC Bank, Delaware, 49 (bottom) LOC, 50 (left) LOC, 52 LOC, 53 LOC, 55 (right) Jerry Irwin, (bottom) DHCA, 56 (top) HSD, 57 (top) HSD, (bottom) Walter Choroszweski, 58 (left) HSD, (right) NWPA, 59 NWPA, 61 (top) Pennsylvania Historical Museum Commission, State Museum, (bottom) DPA, 63 (bottom) DPA, 64 DPA, 65 DHCA, 66 (bottom) DHCA, 67 DPA, 68 (left) DPA, (right) Lee Snider/CORBIS, 69 Kevin Fleming/CORBIS, 71 University Libraries of Notre Dame, 72 JB, 73 LOC. **Chapter Four:** 76–77 DPA, 78 GR, 80 (top) LOC, 81 (right) HSD, 82 NWPA, 83 LOC, 85 (top) LOC, (bottom) NWPA, 86 (top left) US Mint, (bottom left) DPA, (right) HSD, 87 "The Burning of King George III's Portrait on Dover Green, 1776" by Gayle Porter Hoskins, Courtesy of the University of Delaware Permanent Collection, 88 DPA, 89 HSD, 90 (top) NWPA, (bottom) DPA, 91 DPA, 92 HSD, 93 NWPA, 94 LOC, 96 (top) United States Capitol Historical Society, (bottom, left to right) DPA, Gibbs Smith Archives, HSD, Gibbs Smith Archives, 97 iStock/Christine Balderas, 98 Robert E. Goodier, A.W.S., W.H.S., Courtesy of PNC Bank, Delaware, 99 HSD, 101 Jen Petersen. **Chapter Five:** 102–103 LOC, 104 DPA, 106 DPA, 107 (top) DPA, 109 DHCA, 110 (top) HSD, (left) SS/Holly Kuchera, 111 Winterthur Museum, 112 (top) DPA, (bottom) HSD, 114 (left) HSD, 115 HSD, 116 (top) Hagley, 117 Robert E. Goodier, A.W.S., W.H.S., Courtesy of PNC Bank, Delaware, 118 (right) HSD, 119 (top) HSD, (bottom) Hagley, 120 (top) HSD, 121 HSD, 122 (top) HSD, 123 Hagley, 124 HSD, 125 (center) Granger, 126 Hagley, 127 Hagley, 128–129 Hagley. **Chapter Six:** 132–133 National Park Service, 135 (top) HSD, (bottom) LOC, 136 (top) HSD, (bottom) NWPA, 137 (top) LOC, (center) Granger, (bottom) HSD, 138 HSD, 139 LOC, 140 HSD, 141 (top) LOC, 143 LOC, 145 LOC,

147 (top) HSD, (bottom) LOC, 149 (top) Library Company of Philadelphia, (bottom) University of Delaware Public Relations Office, 150 LOC, 151 Hagley, 152 LOC, 153 (top) LOC, (center) HSD, 154–155 LOC, 156 DPA, 157 LOC, 159 Manuscripts, Archives and Rare Books Division, Schomburg Center for Research in Black Culture, The New York Public Library, Astor, Lenox and Tilden Foundations. **Chapter Seven:** 160–165 LOC, 166–168 Hagley, 169 (center) HSD, (bottom) Hagley, 170 (top) DHCA, (bottom left, bottom right) LOC, (bottom center) DPA, 171 (top) DHCA, (bottom) DPA, 172 DPA, 173 (top) HSD, (bottom) DPA, 174 LOC, 175 Hagley, 176–178 LOC, 180 (left) Peoples Settlement Association, (bottom) LOC, 181–182 LOC, 183 (top) U.S. Department of the Interior, National Park Service, Edison National Historic Site, (bottom) Utah State Historical Society, 184 (top) HSD, (bottom) LOC, 185 LOC. **Chapter Eight:** 188–189 Mark E. Gibson/CORBIS, 190 DPA, 191 Hagley, 192 HSD, 193 (top) DPA, (bottom) Hagley, 194 Courtesy of George Chaloupka, 195 (top) DPA, (center) LOC, 196 (top) LOC, (bottom) DPA, 197 LOC, 198 (left) Hagley, (right) DPA, 199 (center) HSD, (bottom) LOC, 200 (top) LOC, (bottom) HSD, 201 (top) DPA, 202 (top) LOC, (center) DPA, (bottom) HSD, 203 DPA, 205 National Archives, 206 HSD, 207 DA, (bottom) ericcrossan.com, 208–209 HSD, 210 (top) Neville Elder/CORBIS, (center) Sean Adair/CORBIS. **Chapter Nine:** 214–215 Mark Gibson/CORBIS, 216 SS/Michele Perbellini, 217 SS/Aaron, 218 (top) iStock/Andre Nantel, (bottom) National Archives, 219–212 JB, 223 (top) DPA, 224 Dean Conger/CORBIS, 225 (top) DPA, 226–227 JB. **Chapter Ten:** 232–233 Ed Eckstein/CORBIS, 235 SS/GeoM, 236 iStock/Sean Locke, 238–239 JB, 241 SS/Alan Smillie, 242 GR, 243 SS/Jennifer Longley, 244 (top) SS/Keith Muratori, (bottom) SS/Jason Smith, 245 Ed Eckstein/CORBIS, 247–248 Kevin Fleming/CORBIS, 249 (top) DTO, (bottom) SS/David Kay, 251 SS/Scott Maxwell.